# Lost with Directions

## Ambling Around America

Rob Erwin

To adventurers everywhere

All over America today people would be dragging themselves to work, stuck in traffic jams, wreathed in exhaust smoke. I was going for a walk in the woods. I was more than ready for this.

— Bill Bryson,  A WALK IN THE WOODS

# PROLOGUE

*"WELC'M TO* Hartford, Tennessee. *Wheres the only thing higher'n the mountains . . . is the locals!"* he said laughing wildly.

A disheveled, middle-aged man with a thick Southern drawl, it had been hard to understand him, but I'd managed to piece it together. He didn't seem high, but his wobbly legs and one whiff of his putrid breath left little doubt he was spectacularly drunk.

Introducing himself as Glenn, he explained that he'd just been kicked out of the bar across the street for bringing in his own twelve-pack of Busch Light. He still didn't understand the big deal. In his words, he was "jus' theres to have a good time."

But here on the porch of the town's BP gas station, Glenn was welcome to drink as much of his own beer as he wanted.

In fact, as I observed, hanging out at the gas station without a thing in the world to do other than drink beer seemed to be the pastime of quite a few of Hartford's 814 residents. It was at this community gathering spot where my friend, Kory, and I had decided to stop at the Pigeon River Smokehouse. Located inside the gas station, it spoke to us after a long day of rafting, hiking, and cliff-jumping in nearby Great Smoky Mountains National Park. On top of that, it appeared to be the only place in Hartford to actually get a hot meal.

Ordering our food at the counter inside, we chose to forego the indoor dining area, which consisted of plastic tables and chairs wedged tightly in between the beverage coolers and the potato chips aisle, and instead opted for fresh air and a picnic table outside where we took in a beautifully warm Tennessee evening.

While Kory sat down, I hustled back to the car and grabbed the two mason jars of apple pie moonshine I'd brought along to celebrate our trip.

"Whatcha got there?" asked Glenn, pointing down at the jar as I returned.

"Some apple pie moonshine," I replied proudly.

"Mine if I has a sip?"

Now this took me off guard. I certainly wasn't inclined to share my drink with a complete stranger, let alone one who was drunk and clearly in need of a bath. It was in this brief moment of hesitation, however, that Kory, who to this point had conveniently remained out of the conversation, decided to chime in.

"Yeah, have some of his," he said, reaching across the table and sliding my jar towards Glenn.

Reacting quickly to pull it away before he could grab it, I politely told Glenn I didn't think it was such a good idea.

*"Whys not?"* he asked crossly with something that resembled a growl. *"You thinks you're too good fer me, like them assholes 'cross the street?!"*

*No, you lunatic. I just don't want you putting your nasty mouth on my drink,* I thought to myself.

"Of course not, Glenn! If you want to go inside the gas station and grab a cup from the soda machine, I'll be happy to pour you some," I said, hoping he would just go away.

As he went off and disappeared, our food soon arrived – a deliciously greasy assortment of brisket, chicken, and ribs, which Kory and I happily devoured. We attempted to sip on our moonshine as well, but to be honest, it was a pretty tough drink to swallow. With the aroma of rubbing alcohol and a taste to match, I couldn't possibly see the appeal of it, let alone understand how so many people in this part of the country could drink it almost religiously.

Speaking of a religious devotion to alcohol, right on cue, Glenn reappeared at our table excitedly tapping me on the shoulder.

"I foun' me's a cup," he said, giggling with delight.

But this was no ordinary cup. In a stroke of divine inspiration, Glenn had instead torn in half one of his Busch Light cans and created a dangerously jagged, makeshift container which he now held out in front of me.

"You's gonna pour me some 'shine?"

"Uh . . . yeah, sure Glenn," I replied hesitantly. But all I could do was stare at the razor sharp aluminum edges of the torn can.

Apparently, Kory was thinking the same thing.

"Are you sure you want to drink from that thing?" he asked with concern. "I mean, it looks pretty sharp . . . I thought you were going to go inside and get a cup from the soda machine?"

*"They's wouldn' lemme inside, so's now this is my goddamn cup!"* Glenn shouted angrily, spittle flying from his mouth and landing in the form of tiny droplets on Kory's face.

"Alright, man, no problem . . ." Kory replied, hastily wiping away the unwelcomed saliva and putting his hands in the air as if to say he'd meant no harm.

For some reason though, his comment had pushed Glenn over the edge.

*"Is my cup not good 'nough for youuuuu?!"* he now screamed furiously, wildly waving the torn-in-half can near Kory's head like a knife. The fading sunlight glinted off the exposed edge as if it were a switchblade. *"You thinks you're better'n meee?!*

It was now readily apparent this guy was on the crazy end of bipolar – for all I knew, he was about to try to slice Kory's face off with the thing.

*"Glenn! Stop!"* I interjected loudly to divert his attention away. He spun around to face me with the look of someone who was deranged.

"How about you just set down the can . . . and we can talk . . ." I said slow and soothingly, sounding like a hostage negotiator trying to de-escalate an out-of-control situation.

"If you set it down on the table . . . we can forget this whole thing ever happened . . . and I'll pour you a nice glass of 'shine . . . Okay?"

He paused to take a long, deep breath, seeming to consider my offer. Quite suddenly, he appeared to shift out of his manic state.

"Well, okays, thats sounds more like it," he replied still a bit smugly, but apparently satisfied. "I mean, we's friends affer'all, right?"

*Right* . . . I thought.

With no intention of drinking anymore of the moonshine, I filled his torn-up can all the way to the brim and watched as his eyes opened wide with surprise. Thanking me profusely, he began stumbling off the porch, managing to spill at least half of it on himself before making it even ten feet away.

*"Enjoys th' Smokies!"* he called out to us happily as he raised the cup in the air, spilling most of the rest of it down his arm.

If the last few minutes with Glenn were any indication, it was going to be an interesting couple of weeks ahead.

# Part 1

## Smoky Mountains

# 1.

**THE ROAD** to Hartford and the path that led me to Glenn had begun several months earlier.

After devoting the past seven years of my life to a modestly successful career coaching small-college football, I'd left behind my current position in South Dakota and returned to Davenport, Iowa, on the banks of the Mississippi River. I was about to be married to my beautiful fiancé, Kellie, whom I'd met there two years earlier. The timing for a career change had been right. I was burnt out, looking for something new, and ready to stop the relentless pattern of job-hopping around the country so common in the profession.

Now, for the first time in my life, I was about to have a nine-to-five office job like everyone else. Unsure of what to expect, I at least took comfort in the fact that, by all accounts,

I'd landed a pretty sweet gig – good pay, lots of free meals, tons of flex-time. Heck, they'd even thrown in free housing. In almost every way possible, it was the ideal situation.

Except that four months later, I was utterly *miserable*.

It didn't take long for me to realize that life in an office constantly checking email, attending meeting after pointless meeting, and wearing khaki pants and a lame dress shirt to work every day was not for me. Quickly becoming frustrated by the mundanity of my work, dejected by the lack of excitement, and in mild despair as I look forward to a future cycling through the same meaningless routine, I was above all else disillusioned by the fact that the people I worked with seemed to think that *all of this was normal*.

I abruptly quit, never to return.

And so it was, in the immediate aftermath, that I decided to hit the road that summer. Nothing major, just something far enough away to be able to clear my head for a couple of weeks while I figured out what to do next. I ran the plan by Kellie, who thought it was a great idea. Most women wouldn't be so supportive of their soon-to-be husband taking off across America just a month before their wedding, but God bless her, she just gets me.

Excited about something for the first time in months, I busily went about researching potential destinations and spent countless hours and late nights on the internet and Google Maps toiling over the task of creating the perfect itinerary. In a country as vast as the U.S. the possibilities were endless, and, in many ways, the process of selecting just a handful of places to go proved to be a daunting task. But after much deliberation, I finally emerged with a plan.

Having spent the past few months working in a sterile, fluorescent-lit, windowless office, I reasoned that perhaps a little time in the great outdoors might be just what I needed to get recharged and re-inspired. Taking two weeks on the road, I would immerse myself in four of America's most iconic wild places: the rolling Smoky Mountains of the Appalachians, the world's first national park at Yellowstone, the most breathtaking valley in America at Jackson Hole, and the high-altitude wonderland that is Rocky Mountain National Park in Colorado.

Hiking the backcountry, camping in the elements, sleeping under the stars, living with the wildlife – the goal wasn't to have a vacation, the goal was to have an adventure.

And now with a plan in place, there was just one thing left to do – hit the road.

2.

**IT HADN'T** taken much to convince Kory, my soon-to-be best man, to come along for the first leg of my journey to the Smoky Mountains in eastern Tennessee and western North Carolina. A lifelong friend since we'd begun playing soccer together when we were ten years old, the two of us had subsequently attended high school and later college together, where we'd mostly bonded over our pathetic inability to get girlfriends.

Now married and working at a bank, talking with him lately, it seemed as if he was in just as much need of a little adventure as I was. From his apartment in suburban St. Louis, it was roughly an eight-hour drive to the Smokies. I could pick him up after he got off work on a Friday, and together we could drive through the night to Tennessee.

Operating on a shoestring budget, I'd gotten the cheapest vehicle the rental agency had to offer – a 2015 Fiat economy car. Comically small and with an absurd bright aqua-blue paint job, it looked as if I'd gotten it on loan from an eccentric clown at Barnum & Bailey rather than the folks from the local Enterprise.

"What the hell is *this*?" asked Kory as I pulled up to the curb outside his apartment.

"This is our ride, man! Get on in," I said, honking the high-pitched horn at him with excitement. It made the same *beep beep* sound the Roadrunner used to make in the old cartoons.

He didn't look amused. "Are you kidding me? I'm not getting in this fucking thing . . ."

"Well, hey man, we could always walk to Tennessee. But I can't guarantee we'll make it on time for our rafting trip tomorrow morning . . ."

"Now hurry up. We're already running late!" I said, revving the engine.

Rolling his eyes, he relinquished and reluctantly threw his things in the trunk. The two of us were on our way to Tennessee.

\*     \*     \*

**ALONG THE** way we had great fun in the typical fashion that any two male friends have on a road trip – crude humor and distasteful jokes. Mostly this involved poking fun at the stereotypes that Northerners have of Southerners. You know, things like inbreeding with your relatives and cannibalizing tourists that get stranded in your small town . . . stuff like that. You have to realize that for people who grew up in the

Midwest, anywhere south of the Mason-Dixon Line is a strange and foreign world to us. You'll have to forgive us if our imaginations run wild a bit.

But by the time we pulled into the Super 8 parking lot at our stopping-off point in the tiny town of Kingston, Tennessee, we had long since run out of things to laugh or joke about. It was 2:30 in the morning, and we were damn tired.

But as luck would have it, it wouldn't be easy getting to bed that night. Grabbing our duffle bags and sleepwalking our way into the underwhelming motel lobby, we discovered to our dismay that there was no attendant on duty. No worries, surely someone was just in the backroom dozing off (I knew I would be at this hour). So we rang the bell at the front desk, but even after several minutes, no one showed.

Now dialing the motel number from my cell phone, I hoped that wherever this guy was, he would surely be compelled to answer the cordless phone motel attendants always carry with them when they wander. But after half-a-dozen calls, still nothing.

Letting our predicament sink in for a moment, we now slowly resigned ourselves to the sad fate that we were going to be forced to sleep in the car for the night. As far as we could tell, this was the only place in town, and we were much too far away from anywhere else to continue on at this late hour.

A night in the Fiat was going to be particularly unpleasant for two reasons: first, the seats wouldn't recline back because there was literally no back seat. And second, we were going to be sleeping in a sparse motel parking lot, located in a small Southern town, smackdab in the middle of nowhere. All of this coming right after we'd spent the majority of the ride down here incessantly joking that these were the types of places where visitors end up disappearing and being eaten by the locals. It was a discomforting thought. Clearly, karma was punishing us for our disparaging remarks on the fine people of the South.

Arriving back to the car, we prepared for the long, uncomfortable night ahead. But in a stroke of luck, just as we were about to close the doors, we noticed a lone man walk out of one of the rooms about three-quarters of the way down the building. We stared at him, and he stared back at us, as he slowly walked along the edge of the motel all the way up to the front entrance. Holding the door open, he called out to us from across the way.

*"You guys here for a room?"*

*Thank God,* I thought, exhaling with relief.

Walking back in the building, we immediately noticed that one thing was very different about the lobby from how it had been just moments earlier – the whole place suddenly reeked as if someone had just smoked about a kilo of marijuana. Considering the only thing to change in the room since we'd last been there was the man standing behind the front desk, it didn't take much to put two and two together. He apologized for not having been there earlier, making up some excuse about having to "fix a TV" in one of the rooms.

Had he been smoking a bowl down there? Definitely. Was there a prostitute involved? Probably. Was that prostitute his cousin? Well, I suppose there's a chance. But at the moment, Kory and I couldn't have cared less. We just desperately wanted to get a few hours' sleep before hitting the road again at seven in the morning.

Had we gotten back to the car ten seconds earlier, we would have missed him entirely. But as it was, we'd gotten lucky, and we were immensely grateful for it that night as we slept soundly in our motel beds instead of the cramped quarters of the Fiat.

3.


**FEELING NOWHERE** near rested, Kory and I rolled out of bed early the next morning and finished the remaining hour-and-a-half drive to Hartford, Tennessee, where we were booked for a morning whitewater rafting excursion with a local outfitter. In no time at all, we were checked in, receiving our gear, and being herded with dozens of others onto a fleet of whitewashed 1970s-era school busses that would act as our shuttle to the launch point some twenty minutes away on the upper Pigeon River.

Arriving at our drop-in spot near a large dam, we made our way past a road sign that read *North Carolina State Line* as we hauled the inflatable red rafts down a short ramp to the water. Beautifully scenic and surrounded by lush, green Southern pines and rocky banks, the Pigeon River was absolutely gorgeous. But it was also a tad underwhelming – in fact, very underwhelming. Peaceful and serene, this looked nothing at all like the Class III and IV rapids I'd seen advertised online on the company website.

But my concerns of false advertising were quickly erased by our guide, Pete, a seasoned rafter in his young-thirties from the nearby mountain-hippie mecca of Asheville. According to him, we were moments away from the folks at the dam transforming this peaceful stretch of river into a roaring water cannon.

"Man, this is going to be pretty rad," he said in a dialect that was a cross between a Southerner and a Malibu surfer. "Are you bros stoked to be here for opening day?"

"What do you mean 'opening day'?" I asked curiously.

"Today's the first day all year they're opening up the dam. People come from all over to be here for it."

Sure enough, already on the river were close to a dozen adventurous kayakers lying in wait for the onslaught of water that was about to come.

"After they release the water, we're going to wait about fifteen minutes before we push off into the current," he added. "By that time, the river's going to be about four feet higher and all those rocks you see out there will all be underwater. And then we're basically just gonna ride the wave, my man. Should be pretty gnarly . . ."

Wearing our matching bright red helmets and life vests, meant to make it easier for Pete to find us if and when we were hurled into the river, Kory and I anxiously watched and waited for the water to rise.

\*     \*     \*

*"TWO LEFT"* called out Pete, issuing his rowing commands to our group of six while he sat perched in back.

*"Two forward! Two more!"* he shouted as we attacked our first rapids of the day and catapulted into whitewater.

Like sitting in the first three rows for the Shamu show at Sea World because you want to get wet, Kory and I had volunteered for the front of the raft. As we barreled through the churning river, we immediately found ourselves soaked to the bone in cold mountain water no more than sixty seconds after we'd launched from shore.

Making it through the initial gauntlet, we soon passed underneath the famed Appalachian Trail, whose 2,200-mile journey from Georgia to Maine goes directly through the Smokies and crosses the Pigeon River at a modest concrete bridge. Made famous by author Bill Bryson in his bestselling 1997 book, *A Walk in the Woods*, it attracts thousands of would-be thru-hikers every year, who spend anywhere from five to seven months traversing the path by foot from end to end. Personally, I much preferred gently floating underneath.

It was here that Pete began to fill us in on the obstacles that lie ahead downstream, including an array of rapids with imposing names like *Full-o-Water*, *Lost Guide*, *Razorblade*, and *Double Reactionary*.

"We used to have one called the *Meat Grinder*," he threw in as a bit of a sidebar. "But we had some guests complain saying it was too graphic, or something. So now it's called *Vegematic*, after a vegetable slicer. Figured no one could complain about that . . ."

All of this led me to consider the very real possibility that I might soon be thrown from the raft and into the river. Not long ago, a spill in the Pigeon River would have been an extremely dangerous prospect – not because of the rocks or rapids, but due to the ungodly levels of toxic waste flowing throughout.

Sadly, this is not a new problem for American waterways. My hometown Mississippi River is amongst the worst in America, with over 12 million pounds of toxic chemicals spewed into it annually. But even by these standards, the Pigeon River had been *bad*. Known as the "Dirty Bird" to locals, as the whitewater conservation group American Whitewater described it, "The Pigeon was for many years so polluted that it was *biologically dead*. The river ran a coffee brown for most of the 20th century, containing toxic chemicals such as dioxins, furan, and chloroform . . ."

Sounds pleasant, right?

All of this toxic runoff had stemmed from a paper mill in the nearby town of Canton. But luckily, by the mid-nineties, the mill had finally started to clean up its act and modernize its production methods. Now, decades later, after tremendous restoration efforts, the water is once again pristine, clean, full of fish, and has been for quite some time now.

Thus, after successfully navigating the Pigeon's many rapids (though I was temporarily launched from my seat and suspended in midair at one point during the *Double Reactionary*) I had no problem jumping overboard with everyone else into the cold, refreshing river for a little float beside the raft as we passed through peaceful waters near the end of our journey.

# 4.

**MOST PEOPLE** don't realize how popular Great Smoky Mountains National Park is, especially if you aren't from the East. As it stands, the Smoky Mountains are far and away the most visited national park in America with nearly 10.7 million visitors annually. That's more than the next two (Grand Canyon at roughly 5.5 million and Rocky Mountain at 4.1 million) combined. This mostly has to do with its close proximity to the highly populated Eastern Seaboard, and doesn't even include the additional 11 million more visitors who come to the nearby gateway towns of Gatlinburg and Pigeon Forge but technically don't enter the park. The entire region is basically a madhouse.

And here were Kory and I on Memorial Day weekend – prime time for the chaos. But in spite of the throngs of tourists sure to be descending upon the park's most popular destinations in its west and central sections, few of these visitors ever make it out to the remote, far northeastern corner of the Smokies, which borders the Cherokee National Forest. Practically speaking, in comparison to the rest of the park, it is all but forgotten. This is where we would go to explore the mountains.

It was difficult enough just getting to the trailhead for Mt. Sterling, one of the taller peaks in this corner of the park at just over 5,800 feet. Exiting the interstate and making our way on ill-maintained backcountry mountain roads, the journey was excruciatingly slow, bumpy, narrow, and winding. Add in a handful of blind hairpin turns only wide enough for one vehicle at a time, and it's enough to leave a person in a nervous sweat before ever even setting foot on the trail.

Considering the rough terrain, it's little wonder this section of forest at Mt. Sterling Gap was once a popular hideout for both Union and Confederate deserters of the Civil War over 150 years earlier. (Hell, it would still be impossible to find someone out here.) On the half-hour ride through this lonely stretch off woods, we never once saw another vehicle on the road, and when we finally found the trailhead it was virtually empty, with the exception of just two other cars parked nearby.

In America's busiest national park, on Memorial Day Weekend, we had managed to find an entire mountain almost exclusively to ourselves.

\*     \*     \*

**IT DIDN'T** take long before my t-shirt was sopping wet and uncomfortably adhering to my skin as we trudged upwards along the rocky dirt path. I'd imagined the short two-and-a-half-mile trail would be a leisurely jaunt to the top, but less than a mile in, I was already sweating profusely and any illusions I'd had of a quick and easy hike to the summit were long gone. Now approaching a grueling set of steep switchbacks, I readied myself for the reality that things were only about to get even more difficult.

"You ready for this?" I called out to Kory, who'd been marching behind me.

Hearing no response, I turned around to discover my partner had instead fallen some thirty or forty yards behind. Waiting for him to catch up, I decided it was probably best we take a water break before one of us collapsed and required the other to drag him back down the mountain.

"This is tough shit," said Kory, still huffing and puffing for breath as the two of us sat down and sprawled out in the middle of the trail.

I agreed. Checking my watch, I couldn't believe it had only been twenty minutes since we'd left the car expecting a leisurely walk in the woods.

*   *   *

**SUFFICE IT** to say, after much exhausting effort, we eventually made it to the top of Mt. Sterling and the 80-year-old fire tower that awaited us at the top. Built in 1935 by the Civilian Conservation Corps, FDR's massive public works program in response to the Great Depression, the tower originated as a first line of defense against wildfires back when the park was first created. Today, however, like many other lookout towers throughout the country, it has been abandoned – replaced by modern technologies such as webcams, which have eliminated the need for park rangers to spend long, lonely days looking out across the forests through their binoculars.

Standing next to it, the tower looked much taller than its actual height of 60 feet. On top of that, it also looked pretty rickety and neglected, as if a stiff breeze were all it might take to send the whole massive structure toppling down on itself in a rusted heap of scrap metal. I attempted to discard the image from my mind as the two of us began taking our first steps toward the small lookout cabin at the top.

But when I say that *we* began our climb to the top of the tower, what I really mean to say is that *I* did. Because it was with great surprise that I was about to learn something I had never known about my closest pal of fifteen years – the guy is desperately afraid of heights. (Isn't it nice to know you can still learn new things about old friends?)

Setting down my pack, I began scaling the narrow, zig-zag sets of stairs, careful not to get tetanus as I held onto the rusted railing. Only once I'd reached the halfway point did I look down to find that Kory was still 30 feet below, timidly sitting on the first step.

*"What? Are you scared?"* I shouted down mockingly.

"No!" he shot back defensively. "My calves are killing me. Did you not just go on the same hike up this mountain that I did?"

But the look on his face said it all.

Continuing to climb, things did start to get a little shaky as I approached the top. Making the amateur mistake of looking down, I suddenly felt anxious, and my heart began racing in my chest as I clung onto the railing for stability. I was pretty sure I could feel the structure ever so slightly swaying in the breeze, though it was impossible to tell if this was actually happening or just my nervous imagination playing tricks on me.

Briefly closing my eyes, I forced myself to take a deep, calming breath, which I slowly exhaled before returning my focus to the stairs. Carefully picking up where I left off, I cautiously finished the last flight of steps before climbing into the observation cabin through a narrow open hatch in the floor.

Comprised of splintered wooden floorboards and brown rusted metal, the inside of the cabin was kind of a dump. But those beautiful paned windows and the views outside – those were incredible.

What struck me most were the stunning shades of *green* on the rolling landscape below. You wouldn't think it, but the Smokies are in fact one of the wettest places in the entire United States. With high-elevation sections of the park averaging up to seven feet of rainfall per year, the area annually collects more precipitation than the Florida Everglades. Scientifically speaking, parts of it are actually considered a rain forest.

All of this moisture is also responsible for the signature morning mists, which the Cherokee of the region long ago compared to blue smoke, ultimately leading to the name "Smoky Mountains." But here in the intense afternoon heat, there was no smoke-like mist to be seen. Instead, the intensely green forest was mixed with a beautiful, deep blue sky above, while white clouds cast dark cobalt shadows below. From my perch on top of the mountain, it all reminded me of a terrific watercolor you might see in a museum.

Making my way back down to the ground, I filled Kory in on all that he was missing. Down here the dense tree cover precluded one from seeing out anywhere, and it seemed like a terrible waste of effort for him to climb all the way to the top of the mountain just to stare at a bunch of trees. So rather than being sensitive and understanding of my friend's fears, I instead resorted to the tried and true methods of peer pressure and questioning his manhood to eventually convince him to begrudgingly make the climb with me. Trailing behind, so as to prevent him from suddenly changing his mind and turning around, the two of us slowly and methodically climbed the sets of stairs until finally reaching the lookout cabin at the top of the tower.

Instantly, I could tell it was worth it.

*"Wow, this is amazing . . ."* he said, pressing his face to the windows with wide eyes as he looked below and out into the distance.

I could tell he meant it. And it made me glad I'd forced him up here, even if it was slightly against his will.

# 5.

**RETRACING THE** winding, rough and tumble backroads we'd taken to get to Mt. Sterling in the first place, we managed to get our tiny blue Fiat back down the mountain in one piece and were now en route to our final destination of the day at a nearby mountain oasis known as Midnight Hole.

Thanks to its reputation as one of the most fantastically picturesque swimming and cliff-jumping spots in the Smokies, Midnight Hole is one of the few places in this forgotten section of the park where you might actually run into a crowd. Nonetheless, we had been assured by Pete (our rafting guide from earlier) that a trip was well worth it. He'd also thrown in a pearl of local wisdom.

"Dude, just wait until dinner time when all the tourists are stuffing their faces . . . you'll have the whole place to yourselves. Guaranteed."

Thus, putting off our own dinner, we pulled up to the Big Creek trailhead around six o'clock and set off on a mile-and-a-half trek through the woods. Sure enough, just as Pete had predicted, a small exodus was taking place on the trail as we passed at least a half-dozen other small groups, all of whom appeared to have just come from the swimming hole as evidenced by their swimsuits, beach towels, and ice coolers. Soon, however, we were all alone and in short order descended down a small, unmarked side path to a place I instantly recognized from the pictures I'd seen. A free-falling waterfall framed by enormous mountain boulders, a churning wake of whitewater casting out into a large tranquil pool – this was Midnight Hole.

The only stragglers still remaining were a group of three teenage boys, who themselves were in the process of packing up and leaving. Other than them, the place was completely deserted.

While Kory changed into his swimming trunks, I dug through my pack, throwing out all of the contents before realizing I'd forgotten my own swimwear back in the car. Now forced to strip down to my boxer-briefs, I stood at the edge of the water as the two of us assessed our approach to the absolutely massive boulders on either side of the falls. To get there we would need to wade across the river and climb a steep granite wall before making our way over to a jumping-off spot.

Setting out across the river (Kory temporarily stayed behind to guard our things from the mischievous-looking teenagers) the water was intensely cold as I waded in up to my waist. Stepping lightly, I attempted to limit the sharp shooting pains in the bottom of my feet as I walked barefoot across a craggy bed of large, slick river rocks.

Once across, I arrived at the granite wall and studied it to determine the best approach to the top. Extremely wet and slippery from others climbing throughout the day, there was little doubt one needed to be exceedingly careful here lest they go for a painful and potentially dangerous fall. Cautiously scaling the rocks, I took my time finding the proper toeholds and gradually ascended before pulling myself up and over the final ledge.

In the fading daylight, the water in the pool below was impenetrably dark (hence the name Midnight Hole), and as I stood on the ledge, it was impossible to gauge how deep the water might be or if any more massive stones or boulders lurked beneath the surface. In my head, I knew it was safe – *people jump here all the time,* I told myself. But there was still a certain nervousness and uncertainty in not being able to discern it with my own eyes. As the old saying goes, "seeing is believing," and here I couldn't see a damn thing.

Having stood there a bit too long to contemplate things, the teenagers back on the river banks started giving me a hard time.

"What are you waiting for?" shouted one of the boys.

"Jump in already you *pussy!*" called out another.

*Did some fourteen-year-old punk with braces really just call me a pussy?*

Screw these kids, I was jumping.

Raising my head, I looked out across the way to Kory and without warning catapulted off the ledge, plummeting down towards the dark pool below. Bracing myself for potential impact, I instead crashed through the surface and was immediately engulfed in the numbingly cold water that enveloped my body as I plunged further down. Feeling with my feet for the bottom, it was nowhere to be found.

I'd imagined a surreal underwater scene below, but was instead greeted by complete darkness as I looked out around me – the water so cold it hurt my eyes just to open them. Now, racing for air, I saw the pale light of the surface above me and gasped wildly for breath as I shot above the waterline. Looking back to the shoreline and shouting with excitement, my voice echoed loudly through the rocky cove over the low roar of the waterfall.

A leap of faith – it was the perfect metaphor for all that lie ahead.

# Part 2

# Yellowstone & Tetons

# 6.

**DROPPING OFF** Kory and the Fiat back in St. Louis the following evening, I briefly returned home to Iowa before taking my journey west. Heading out the door on a Wednesday morning, I was already an hour behind schedule due to the fact that I'd been up well past midnight the previous evening packing and double-checking my supplies. (I was still absolutely certain I'd forgotten something important . . . though I had no idea what.)

To save on the exorbitant cost of a two-week rental, I was now in my 2008 red Ford Fusion, which in addition to showing its first signs of rust, had also recently passed the 100,000-mile mark on the odometer. In my past experience with other vehicles, this meant any day now the car was about to have a mid-life crisis and blow a starter, snap an engine belt, or have something else go terribly wrong that would inevitably leave me stranded by the side of the road needing an expensive tow and repair.

I crossed my fingers that it could hang tough for just another 4,000 miles before crapping out on me . . . when we got home, it could literally fall apart for all I cared. But with a roundtrip journey in front of us that exceeded a drive from Key West to Seattle, there was no telling whether we'd actually make it that far.

First things first, was the incredibly long, day-and-a-half drive across the Great Plains to the remote northwest corner of Wyoming.

Yellowstone awaited.

\*     \*     \*

**BY THE** time I made it to Sioux Falls, South Dakota, for dinner, it had already been a long and difficult day on the road. I'd had gas station food for breakfast, more gas station food for lunch, and an assortment of energy drinks along the way . . . all of which left me feeling predictably nauseous for the majority of the drive.

Luckily, the opportunity to get out of the car and have a home-cooked meal was a welcome break to what had thus far been a rough day of travel. I was fortunate that my good friend Jordan, a former colleague from my coaching days and soon-to-be groomsman in my wedding, just so happened to live in Sioux Falls, right off I-90 where I was now passing through.

"So you're going to be out in Yellowstone, in the middle of nowhere, for two weeks . . . by yourself?" he asked as he strained a batch of spaghetti noodles over the kitchen sink.

"Well, I'll only be in Yellowstone by myself for part of the trip. I'm meeting a buddy out in Jackson Hole and then another friend down in Colorado," I clarified.

He seemed to be mulling it over. "Well, did you at least bring a gun?"

"A *gun?*"

"Yeah, a gun," he replied back emphatically, "in case you get attacked out there."

"Why would I get attacked?"

"I don't know, you might run into a crazy person out in the woods. You know that's where crazy people live, out in the woods," he said matter-of-factly, as if it were the most obvious thing in the world.

"And what about bears?" he added. "What are you going to do if a giant grizzly bear walks up on your ass and wants to eat you? I bet you're going to want a gun then."

On this matter, I wasn't concerned. In fact, one of the main reasons I was going out to Yellowstone in the first place was to hopefully see some of the park's incredible wildlife, especially the bears. If anything went awry, I'd be carrying some non-lethal bear spray just in case.

*"Bear spray? Non-lethal? Is that a joke?"* he shot back in disbelief. "Rob, let me tell you about this movie I just watched . . ."

He then proceeded to explain the gory details behind a recent thriller-horror film he'd seen on TV called *Backcountry*, a story about a Canadian couple who goes camping in the wilderness only to be stalked and mauled by a predatory black bear. Apparently, it was based off a real-life incident that took place in Ontario back in 2005.

"When that bear was done with them, it was like this spaghetti and marinara sauce *everywhere*," he said, summing up the gruesome ending to the film as I watched him mix in the red pasta sauce with a large wooden spoon.

My stomach turned at the gory comparison, and suddenly I wasn't quite so hungry.

"So, you still gonna use that weak-ass pepper spray?"

I assured him that I'd be okay, that all of the research out there shows spray is actually the most effective means of defense. But Jordan was having none of it. In his mind, I was already as good as devoured.

"You're crazy," he concluded, as he dolloped a messy serving of the warm spaghetti on my plate.

\*     \*     \*

**CRASHING WITH** a friend for the night in Rapid City in western South Dakota, I was back on I-90 the following morning as I skirted the Black Hills and crossed the state line into Wyoming. Driving through a heavy morning thunderstorm, I stopped to stretch my legs in the town of Sheridan and eat a late lunch before gearing up to exit the interstate and make the daunting climb into the Bighorn Mountains.

It was in the Bighorns where I was worried that my Fusion would blow out its engine cranking RPMs as it ascended the steep switchbacks on the way up and over. Within just a few short miles of climbing, I had already risen so high in the sky that I could see the curve of the earth as I looked out to the immense, flat plains below.

Now entering the interior of the range, it was a distinct sensation of stepping off the grid – cell service disappeared, the GPS stopped working, and if I'd wanted to find my way around I would have actually needed to use a paper map. On top of this, there was an undeniable sense of solitude, as I had the narrow two-lane road entirely to myself for much of the journey. Taking my time to pass through slowly, I allowed myself to enjoy the Bighorns' shifting landscapes from grassy meadows and rolling hills in the east, to red rock canyons and sheer cliffs in the west.

And now arriving on the other side, I could finally sense that my ultimate destination was near. With only 120 miles left to go, in two short hours I would be entering the gates of Yellowstone.

# 7.

**CREATED AS** the world's first national park over 140 years ago, Yellowstone was originally nicknamed *Wonderland* by those who visited for its fantastical, otherworldly array of high-spouting geysers, boiling mudpots, multi-colored hot pools, and superheated fumaroles that cause the earth to literally steam underfoot in places.

Today, however, Yellowstone is equally revered as one of the last remaining intact wilderness ecosystems left on the planet.

And of all the wild residents who call Yellowstone home, perhaps none is more famous than its largest predator, the grizzly bear. As one of only two remaining areas in the Lower 48 that hosts a large population (the Glacier National Park region in northwest Montana being the other) it is no exaggeration to say that virtually every visitor to Yellowstone hopes to see a grizzly at some point on their trip. Unfortunately, this is easier said than done.

Of the roughly 700-800 grizzlies that live in the greater Yellowstone region, only around 150 actually reside within the massive 3,400 square miles that lie within park boundaries (an area larger than the states of Rhode Island and Delaware combined.) So I hate to burst your bubble, but even in Yellowstone, the odds of seeing a grizzly aren't very good.

Of course, this wasn't going to stop me from trying.

*     *     *

**IT'S HARD** to say why I have such a tremendous fascination with animals, but my wife seems to think it has something to do with the fact that I'm an only-child and had "no one to talk to as a kid," as she likes to put it.

I guess this is partially true. Growing up in rural Illinois surrounded by beans and cornfields, there were only two other children within a one-mile radius of my home, and I did in fact spend much of my time socializing with my pet cat, my neighbor's three horses, and occasionally a flea-infested stray dog whom I secretly fed hotdogs to out behind my dad's tractor shed.

At one point as a young child, I had the bright idea to create a "detective club" with these four-legged companions of mine and thought it would be terribly exciting and fun to solve local neighborhood crimes and mysteries like the *Boxcar Children*. Sadly though, like most ideas hatched by an eight year old, it didn't really work out. At our first "meeting," the dog nearly killed my cat and chased it up a tree, and my dad yelled at me for letting the horses out of their pen while he and my neighbor spent the next five hours trying to wrangle them back in.

Okay, so maybe she's right . . . I really did have no one to talk to as a kid.

But regardless of why, it's safe to say that to this day I'm still very much an animal lover. Perhaps this is why I was so dead-set on seeing a grizzly bear. But true to the spirit of my trip, I wasn't much interested in doing it from the front seat of my car or from the side of the road like most tourists. I wanted to get out into their territory, out into the backcountry.

With this in mind, I had hoped to make it to the park early enough to get in a quick hike before dark at the relatively obscure Pelican Valley – the beating heart of Yellowstone grizzly country. Located near the northern edge of the enormous Yellowstone Lake, there is so much bear activity in this small, otherwise un-noteworthy valley, that the trail here is explicitly closed to hikers for several months of the year, and even when it is open, it is highly regulated. And while what I said earlier is true, the odds of seeing a grizzly in Yellowstone are indeed low, the Pelican Valley is undoubtedly one of the best places to look. The other great thing – most tourists don't even know it exists.

Rolling through the park's tollbooth-style East Entrance, I proceeded the final, winding twenty miles to the valley, arriving roughly an hour before dusk. It was just enough time to poke around a little and see if I could get lucky on my first night.

Arriving at the trailhead, I decided now would be a prudent time to learn how to use the bear spray I was relying on to keep me safe in the event things got a little too up close and personal. A small, handheld red container resembling a miniature fire extinguisher, I examined the directions on the side and was relieved to discover that the instructions were pretty straightforward: pull off the safety guard, aim, and spray. Even I couldn't mess that up.

The only potentially tricky part might be getting the safety guard off in the heat of the moment, so I practiced flicking it off with my thumb a few times just to get the hang of it. Feeling confident, I slid it back into my pocket and started out towards the valley. But a few steps later, I stopped in my tracks. *Maybe I should actually practice using this thing,* I thought to myself.

So I followed the directions: I flipped the safety guard, aimed at a tree roughly ten feet away, and pulled the trigger as a massive, high-powered plume of orange spray came firing out the nozzle. This thing was powerful, there was even a bit of a recoil. And then I felt the slightest breeze on my face . . .

*BAM!*

Like taking a whiff of nerve gas, I collapsed to my knees coughing and gagging uncontrollably. Instantly my face was on fire and my eyes burned like white-hot charcoals. My throat was swelling, it was getting harder to breathe, panic was setting in. Writhing in agony, I could taste it in my mouth and frantically spit to rid myself of it as the tears rolled down my face in my body's desperate efforts to flush away the monstrous chemicals.

Helplessly, I continued on in this state of uncontrollable havoc for several more minutes before finally getting a grip.

*Un-fucking believable,* I thought to myself as I recovered along the side of the trail. *Who sprays themselves in the face with their own bear spray?*

Unfortunately, things were only about to get worse.

\* \* \*

**IT WAS** only a quick hike out on the trail, maybe half an hour or so, before it started to get too dark and I was forced to turn around and get back to the car. Suffice it to say, I didn't see any bears. But that was okay, I'd come back early tomorrow morning.

Making my way back along the road to where I'd parked, I was almost to the car when I was approached by a sporty SUV with California plates, which pulled up alongside me and rolled down the passenger window. Inside was a young couple, who from the looks of it had just gotten done with a hike themselves.

"Hey, are you the guy with the red Ford down the road there?" asked the man from across the way in the driver's seat.

"Yeah . . ." I replied hesitantly, unsure and a little worried about why he was asking.

"Oh, good! We just got done hiking Storm Point and saw your car there. It's starting to get pretty dark, and we were worried you might still be out on the trail."

This was a relief. My first concern had been a flat tire.

"Yeah, I'm actually on my way back to the car right now. Thanks for keeping an eye out though, guys. I appreciate it."

"No problem," responded the gal in the passenger seat. "Be careful though, we just saw a fox over by your car!"

Resuming my walk back to the car, it didn't take long

before I saw the canine she'd been referring to. But this couple clearly didn't know their wildlife – because this thing sure as hell wasn't a fox.

Not only did it not have the signature reddish coat of a fox, nor the large bushy tail, but from about forty yards away I could tell this guy was bigger . . . much bigger.

*Holy shit, that's a wolf,* I realized.

Instantly, my heart began racing and my breath became short, as a wave of panic set in throughout my body. My last chance for help had just driven off and out of sight down the road, inexplicably thinking it was a harmless fox. If there ever had been a fox here, it was now in this thing's belly.

Lowering his head, he slowly and deliberately crept towards me. Steadily narrowing the gap between us, he approached curiously, as if he hadn't yet decided what to do with me – eat me all at once, or save part of me for later.

Mouth open, tongue out . . . was he salivating? *Oh shit.*

I reached into my pocket for the bear spray, hoping it would have the same effect on this wolf as it had on me earlier. In spite of shooting myself in the face, I was glad I'd at least practiced using it.

Now less than twenty yards away, my farsighted eyes were finally able to get a good hard look at the animal. Strangely though, all of a sudden he didn't seem quite as big as I'd first thought. And what was with those overly large ears and that long narrow face? I quickly realized I'd been losing my nerve over nothing. This was no wolf in front of me, but merely a coyote.

Letting out a huge sigh of relief, all at once I felt the tension leave my body. It's amazing how your mind can play tricks on you when you're on a dark and lonely road by yourself at night. Now feeling safe, I began walking towards the animal shouting, determined to spook him off. After all, they're more scared of us than we are of them, right?

Wrong.

Soon twenty yards became fifteen, and then fifteen became ten. Nine, eight, seven, six . . . he refused to flee. And again, my heart raced with panic.

*Why is he staring at me like that? Maybe he has rabies.*

*No, he definitely has rabies! Oh God, I'm going to be found naked in the woods, foaming at the mouth like some crazy person.*

Again, I clutched the bear spray and with a flick of my thumb popped off the safety guard and aimed. Sure, I'd probably spray myself in the face again and go through twenty minutes of writhing on the ground coughing and gasping in agony. But it sure as hell beat rabies.

But just then, a pale light flashed in the coyote's eyes, briefly giving him a sinister, demonly look. Approaching from behind, a bright yellow tourist trolley loaded with sightseers had pulled up along the side of the road. In what amounted to absolute perfect timing, they'd somehow been passing by at the exact right moment and had come to my rescue.

Both the coyote and I stopped dead in our tracks and stared at the trolley, waiting to see what would happen next. But to my surprise, the driver didn't blare the horn to scare it off, nor did he get out and try to assist me. Instead, he put the trolley in park . . . and that's when the flashbulbs started going off. The damn tourists were taking pictures of the coyote.

*Are you kidding me?* I thought to myself stunned.

*Do they even see me?*

Of course they did, they just didn't care. Surely, many of them were already imagining how many Facebook "likes" or YouTube views they could get for posting a video of my attack online. I couldn't believe it.

Ears alertly perked, eyes darting back and forth between me and the trolley, the coyote was now clearly just as nervous I was. The two of us stood frozen, yards apart in a game of chicken that neither of us wanted any part of anymore.

The standoff seemed to be dragging on forever when, quite unexpectedly, a speeding vehicle flew by at breakneck speed. The coyote and I had both been so focused on each other that we hadn't heard or seen it coming. Scaring the living hell out of me, I was completely startled and wildly jumped back from the road in panic. Fortunately, however, it did an even greater number on my four-legged adversary who violently recoiled and scurried away.

Finally, there was some distance between the two of us, and I could breathe a little easier.

Now that I was out of harm's way, the tourists had apparently lost interest, and the flashbulbs ceased as the trolley pulled back onto the road and sped away. In turn the coyote, who'd decided this was all just too much stress, slinked into a tall patch of nearby grass and instantly disappeared.

And just like that, I was once again by myself on the road. This short evening hike to the Pelican Valley had turned out to be way more than I'd bargained for.

# 8.

**EVERY SUMMER** over 3,000 seasonal employees flock to Yellowstone from around the country (and around the world) to work in the park's shops, restaurants, and lodges, as they meet the needs of over 4 million visitors. Many of these seasonal workers are retirees, while others are American college students, and still a significant number are international students happy to spend their summers in the U.S.

Occasionally though you get an oddball who doesn't fit into any of these categories, and back in the summer of 2013, that happened to be me. Still working as a college football coach in Illinois for ten months of the year, I had heard from a friend out West about the opportunities available working in Yellowstone for the summer and had decided to apply.

With seasonal workers always in desperately short supply,

I'd quickly been hired and assigned to the junction in the park known as the Fishing Bridge. Located on the northern tip of Yellowstone Lake, at the mouth of the Yellowstone River, the area is fittingly named for the historic wooden bridge that spans the river at this point (though contrary to what you might expect, fishing is actually no longer permitted at the Fishing Bridge, and park rangers will happily pounce on you if you try).

And while I could easily write an entire book about the life-changing experiences that took place for me in those few months, suffice it to say, it was completely transformative and made me fall in love with Yellowstone.

Now, two years later, I was back.

Looking to catch my breath after an unexpectedly stressful visit to the Pelican Valley, I moseyed on down the road several miles before soon finding myself back at the Fishing Bridge, my old, familiar stomping grounds. Driving by I experienced a rush of nostalgia as I passed my old dormitory and witnessed a handful of college kids passing the night away on the covered front porch. Seconds later, I passed the general store where I'd worked in the employee dining room, and the flood of memories continued.

My immediate destination was actually across the street from all of this, at the Fishing Bridge Museum and Visitor Center. An old cabin with a variety of interpretive displays and a small gift shop inside, it had closed over an hour earlier, and the normally crowded parking lot was nothing more than a vacant sea of concrete. But near the front doors, a handful of vehicles remained, and this is where I now pulled in. Walking around the side of the building to the edge of the woods, I approached a cozy amphitheater with wooden benches and a large projection screen in front.

I had arrived for the nightly educational presentation put on here throughout the summer, as the park rangers illuminate the amphitheater with a variety of slideshows related to life in Yellowstone. Back when I'd lived across the street, I had immensely enjoyed these lectures, and now that I was back, it seemed like a perfect way to unwind after a long day.

Tonight's presentation was something to the effect of *Wolves to Weasels: The Amazing Wildlife of Yellowstone.* Obviously, this was right up my alley. Sitting front and center in the first row, like the overeager teacher's pet I'd been since a child, I was greeted by the young female ranger who seemed immensely grateful I'd shown up – I'd brought the attendance from a total of four guests to five. Undeterred by the low turnout, she was exceptionally enthusiastic and put on a terrific lecture, even seeming to solve the mystery of my rabid coyote encounter (apparently, visitors had been tossing food out to them by the side of the road recently, and the animals were now becoming conditioned to beg).

By the time the lecture was over, however, I myself was begging for food. Having not eaten since lunch on the other side of the Bighorns in Sheridan, by this point in the evening, I was positively starving for sustenance. Unfortunately, with the store across the street now closed for the night, any hopes I'd had for a good meal before bed were completely dashed. It looked like the half-eaten bag of Cool Ranch Doritos in the back seat of the car would have to do.

In addition to this, I was just now realizing I had never actually acquired a campsite for the night. Sure, I could go down the road another five miles and do a walk-in registration at the Bridge Bay campground, but honestly, by this point in the day, I was so exhausted that the thought of having to unload my gear and set up camp seemed too tiring to even think about.

Instead, I went with my backup plan.

Located on the pristine shores of the water, resembling a massive Southern plantation-style mansion picked up and dropped into the heart of the Wyoming wilderness, the Lake Yellowstone Hotel dates back well over a hundred years when it was built to house the influx of wealthy Eastern tourists coming to the park via the newly constructed railways through the West. Painted a subdued pastel yellow and beautifully beset with enormous ornate white columns, in the daylight it is a remarkable piece of architecture which pulls off the rare feat of somehow actually managing to enhance its incredible natural surroundings. Staying true to tradition, however, just as it was in the old days, the hotel remains a pricey place to lay your head at night. And at two hundred dollars per evening, a posh room wasn't exactly in my trip budget.

Instead, I pulled the Fusion into a vacant spot in the crammed parking area, turned off the engine, and reclined the driver's side seat. Tonight I would have to enjoy the hotel's luxurious elegance from afar. Due to strict nighttime light restrictions in the park, meant to reduce light pollution and ensure the visibility of dazzling starry skies, the lot was nearly pitch-black, and the beautiful building itself eerily dark save for a few guestrooms emitting a dim golden glow inside. Tucked away discreetly in my car, it would be the perfect place to grab some shuteye for the night and recover from an unexpectedly chaotic first evening in Yellowstone.

# 9.

**I AWOKE** in my car around 4:30 a.m. to a world that was uninvitingly dark and gray in the early morning dawn. I had not slept soundly at all. In the middle of the night, I'd awoken from my sleep shivering with cold as the temperature outside had fallen drastically. Getting out of the car, I rummaged through the trunk to haul out my sleeping bag, insert myself inside, and zip up as I attempted to warm my body temperature. Still overcome with chill, I turned on the car engine and cranked up the heat. When I awoke to my alarm several hours later, the car was still on and idling.

Now making the short drive back up the road for the Pelican Valley, I could see my breath as I step out into the cold, uncomfortable chill of the early morning air and donned a thick winter jacket and old stocking cap for warmth. Still groggy and half-asleep, I set out on a slow walk along the currently deserted stretch of road towards the trail.

I took solace in one fact – this early morning hour was absolutely prime time to spot a bear. Grizzlies, like many animals in the park, are particularly active during the early morning hours of dawn. Sure, I was cold, hungry, and sleep deprived, but I'd done the hard part of getting up early while everyone else in Yellowstone was still sound asleep. Slowly starting to come awake as I approached the trailhead, I felt a quiet confidence that my efforts would be rewarded.

*     *     *

**THREE HOURS** later, I emerged from the valley sweaty, dirty, tired, and without even the slightest hint of a bear sighting. Instead, I'd spent the majority of my hike exerting vast amounts of energy hiking off-trail in order to appease a handful of particularly ornery bison who hadn't fully appreciated my early morning visit.

Don't get me wrong, I love the fact that Yellowstone is teeming with thousands of bison – they're a symbol as synonymous with the West as cowboys, and their comeback in the park is a tremendous story worth telling.

Once dominating the Great Plains and valleys of the Mountain West in numbers perhaps as high as 60 million, most Americans still remember from history class that the bison were nearly hunted to the point of extinction during the period of American westward expansion. And while at one time these massive herds literally shook the earth and rumbled like thunder as they ran across the plains, by the late 1890s the plains had gone silent. Not a single wild bison remained in America, save for a small depleted herd which clung to survival right here in the Pelican Valley of the nation's newly created national park at Yellowstone. But with illegal poaching rampant during the park's early years, even here they weren't safe. By the time the government cracked down on the problem and got things under control, only *twenty-three* bison remained of the original 60 million.

Fortunately though, after over a century of protection and recovery, the bison are back in Yellowstone to the tune of nearly 5,000. In fact, it seems like they're everywhere you look. Back during the summer of 2013, when I'd just entered the park for the first time and was reporting for work, I became stalled in one of the area's famous "bison jams." It's a phenomenon where several hundred of these massive, shaggy brown beasts engulf the roadway and bring traffic to a complete standstill, sometimes for miles. Like a large lazy river, unperturbed by a few rocks in its path, the herd slowly lumbered around the stopped vehicles while passengers inside excitedly took pictures and shot videos.

Coming within inches of my car, I could very literally smell their warm, dank breath as they walked by my driver's side window, and I seriously contemplated whether or not my insurance would cover any scratches left behind by their horns. Turning the engine off while I waited, I listened to the chorus of clattering hooves on the pavement until the last one had passed by. It was quite the welcome to Yellowstone.

But this morning, out on the trail in the Pelican Valley, I experienced the less pleasant side of these normally docile creatures – namely the fact that they can become extremely territorial and aggressive when they feel their personal space is being invaded. Having been on the trail for a couple miles, I happened to stumble upon a small group lazily lounging about in their large, dusty daybeds alongside the trail. Bathing in the sun, they seemed to be spending the majority of their time using their whip-like tails to swat at the pestering flies that landed on their enormous backsides.

With several dozen of them scatted about the path as I emerged from the woods and into the open valley, I attempted to give them a wide berth by making large arcs around the spots on the trail where they were congregated. Skeptical of my good intentions, however, they eyed me suspiciously even as I found myself trudging through ankle-deep water and mud in a wet, marshy lowland. From their comfortable position on the high ground next to the trail, they continued to watch me wearily. And now as I look around, I realized there were only two ways ahead – either get back on the trail, or continue sloshing around through this unpleasant swamp.

I wondered if perhaps I wasn't being a bit overcautious. Maybe I just needed to show a little assertiveness instead (you know, because that same line of reasoning had worked so well with the coyote the night before).

Once again, big mistake.

Taking just a few small steps out of the mud and back towards the trail, an enormous, hulking bull erupted from his wallow and jolted to a defensive, upright position. Violently shaking the dirt off his back, he stood in the ensuing cloud of dust like an apparition, glaring at me menacingly while daring me to take a single step further.

*"What the hell is your problem?"* I shouted out angrily in

frustration, as if I might somehow break the language barrier and reason with him.

Now snorting and huffing loudly, he responded in turn by lowering his horns and angrily pawing at the ground. Instantly, I froze at the unmistakable threat of a charge. I regretted losing my cool and wished I'd just kept my mouth shut. He might not have understood what I'd said, but he clearly hadn't liked my tone.

"Fine, I'm leaving . . ." I muttered under my breath bitterly, this time slowly backing away.

So far on my trip, my encounters with park wildlife had been anything but safe. The way things were going, a grizzly sighting might not turn out very well for me.

*Maybe I should just look for animals by the side of the road like everyone else,* I thought to myself as I turned and defeatedly began sulking my way back to the trailhead.

\*    \*    \*

**MY BREAKFAST** of bacon, eggs, hashbrowns, and pancakes back at the Fishing Bridge came as a much needed source of satisfaction after a rough morning on the trail. It was the first decent sit-down meal I'd had since dinner with Jordan two days ago in Sioux Falls, and it did much to lift my spirits after the less-than-friendly encounter I'd had with the bison of the Pelican Valley.

But now with my stomach full, I longed for another welcome comfort to any weary traveler – a hot shower. Without a change of clothes since Rapid City, and with two hikes under my belt out in the valley, I was dirty enough to resemble the kid from Charlie Brown who has that cloud of dirt following him wherever he goes. On top of that, I was still carrying the pungent aroma of bear spray with me like a bad cologne.

But getting a hot shower in Yellowstone is something easier said than done. Seeing as I wasn't a guest at the Lake Hotel and the nearby RV campground was filled to capacity, my two primary options weren't really options at all. Sure, I could have found a quiet, secluded spot somewhere to take a skinny dip in the lake or the river to wash off the dirt and grime, but considering both sources of water had only recently thawed from their winter freeze (it is often typical for Yellowstone Lake to remain frozen until late May or early June) these didn't really seem like options either.

For most visitors, it would be tough-out-of-luck situation. Fortunately for me, I knew of one more place to go.

Returning to the car, I grabbed a fresh change of clothes, some shampoo, a towel, and crammed them into a black nylon knapsack. Donning a pair of dark sunglasses and pulling my ball cap low over my brow, I stealthily approached my old dormitory building as if I were about to sneak into a highly classified government facility.

I knew that at this time of day, around 11:30 in the morning, just about everyone would be working over at the store, and the odds of encountering someone were low. Indeed, climbing the stairs of the front porch and walking into the foyer, I found the cabin completely empty. Resisting the petty urge to take a peek inside my old room across the hall, I made a quick right turn towards the communal bathroom, shut the door, and immediately began to disrobe.

I knew from experience that, if I was lucky, the dormitory showers were good for about exactly one minute's worth of hot water. This was far from a luxury resort – the building had first been constructed almost 90 years ago, and I seriously doubt if any significant renovations or repairs have been made since then. Now standing wrapped in my towel, keeping constant vigil for someone to walk in and catch me as a trespasser, I turned on the shower and waited for the frigid water to slowly warm past freezing.

The moment it turned lukewarm, I discarded the towel and bolted inside. The sixty-second countdown was on, and time was ticking fast. Racing to beat the clock, I lathered up the Old Spice body wash and successfully rinsed off like a seasoned veteran.

Thirty seconds left . . . I could do this.

Reaching for the Suave shampoo though, I started to panic as I could already feel the water temperature starting to fade. Losing my nerve, I carelessly fumbled the bottle in my hands sending it crashing to the floor.

Twenty seconds . . . I was never going to make it.

Ten seconds . . . I tried rinsing the bubbles out of my hair, but it was too late. The water was too cold, and I couldn't take it any longer. Already shivering, I turned the shower knob to end the torture.

Hastily drying off and throwing on a fresh set of clothes, I slowly opened the creaky bathroom door, poked my head around the corner to confirm the coast was clear, and quickly rushed out of the old cabin undetected back to my car.

After less than a day in Yellowstone, it was already time to hit the road again. And to tell the truth, I couldn't have been happier.

# 10.

**NEEDING TO** hit the reset button on my trip and get things back on track, I was now back in the car and heading two hours south down to Jackson, Wyoming, where I'd be meeting my oldest friend in the world, Jake, for a couple nights of camping in Grand Teton National Park.

Jake and I have known each other ever since the first day of kindergarten. Noticing the embarrassingly bad lazy eye I had as a child, he'd innocently tapped me on the shoulder and asked if I was *"retarded."* Not knowing what this meant, I simply replied, "I think so?"

Somehow, the two of us have been friends ever since.

Today, Jake is the most accomplished world traveler I know. He's one of those types who randomly decides to go to Ireland, or maybe Buenos Aires for the weekend, simply because he's bored and has nothing else better to do. He's camped in the Sahara Desert, gone on safari, climbed to Machu Picchu, road-tripped through Australia, walked the countryside of Cambodia, and that just scratches the surface of what he's done in the past year or two. His exploits are far too many to name, and the stamps in his passport book would put just about anyone to shame.

Oh, and I almost forgot to mention – he has perks with a major airline to fly anywhere in the world, at any time, for absolutely *free*. Jealous? Me too.

I was excited he had chosen to come out to Wyoming with me when he could have literally gone anywhere in the world with his weekend off. And if he deemed my little expedition exciting enough for him to tag along, I wanted to make sure it lived up to his expectations. For this reason, we had planned to stay the first night in the backcountry, off the beaten path, where we could get a true and authentic taste of the Teton wilderness.

Leaving Fishing Bridge, I began the drive down to Yellowstone's South Entrance where I exited the park and entered the John D. Rockefeller Parkway, a public tract of land which connects Yellowstone to the north and Grand Teton to the south.

It was at this time I realized I didn't have much in the way of a game plan once Jake arrived – heck, I still didn't even know where we were going to camp that night. Not wanting my friend to fly all the way from Chicago to Wyoming only to realize that we had nowhere to stay because of my lack of planning, I pulled over to the side of the road to evaluate potential campsites for the evening.

I couldn't have picked a more idyllic spot to park. Just as the highway continues south through the Rockefeller and dips into the northern section of Grand Teton, the road rounds the bend and it's here for the first time that one is presented with the staggering Teton Range as it abruptly rises into the sky. Towering over the immaculate Jackson Lake, my eyes couldn't help but be drawn to the massive translucent reflection of Mount Moran as it shown upside down in the mirror-like waters below. Within a stone's throw of the water's edge, this was where I got out of the car.

Sitting down on an enormous slab of rock on the shoreline, I slipped off my shoes and dipped my toes down into the icy water as I pulled out a backcountry map for the park. When it came to campsites, Jake and I were in a bit of a predicament. His flight's arrival had already been pushed back an hour to seven o'clock this evening, and we were going to be hard pressed to get just about anywhere before the sun went down. And in grizzly country, we definitely wanted to be off the trail by dark (I wanted to see a bear more than anybody, but I didn't want to do it by hiking through the mountains blind as a bat and then accidentally running into something large and furry).

Scanning the map, I quickly discovered that we very literally had just *one* viable option in the entire park if we had any hope of arriving with a shred of daylight. Identified by a small triangle marking on the map, a campsite along the shoreline of diminutive Phelps Lake was our only hope. It had a few things going for it, the most important of which was the fact that the trailhead to get there was perhaps just twenty-five minutes from the Jackson Hole Airport. On top of this, it was only a relatively short three-mile hike to the campsite. Could we make it there before dark? Who knew? But at this point, it was the only shot we had.

*     *     *

**HOPPING BACK** in the car, I made the short trip down to the Colter Bay Visitor Center where I crossed my fingers and prayed that the site at Phelps Lake was still available and hadn't already been reserved. If it had already been snatched up, we were going to be royally screwed.

Fortunately, we were in luck.

"Actually, there are three sites down at Phelps Lake, and it looks like two of them are available," said the friendly, middle-aged woman at the backcountry office.

I breathed a sigh of relief.

Registering the site and paying the camping fee, I was required to watch an informational video on backcountry rules, regulations, and safety precautions before she could finally sign off on the reservation. It mostly consisted of the standard stuff: bring enough water, don't litter, don't burn down the forest, et cetera. But then it got to bear safety.

"When hiking alone or in small groups, be off the trail by dark . . ." it warned gravely.

I hoped more than ever that Jake's flight would get in early.

*     *     *

**CONTINUING SOUTH** towards the Jackson Hole Airport, I now marveled out the windshield as I passed the namesakes of the Teton Range – South Teton, Middle Teton, and the Grand Teton itself, with its distinct leaning summit at nearly

14,000 feet. Standing tall over the serpentine bends of the Snake River below, the peaks were originally named by early French fur trappers. Apparently lonely for the comforts of women, they dubbed them *les trois tetons*, which literally translates to mean "the three breasts." (Obviously, months on end of trapping muskrats and beavers alone up in the mountains can do things to a man.)

And while there are certainly higher peaks in America, there are few quite so spectacular. Resembling a row of serrated, razor-sharp shark's teeth biting at the sky, the range's absence of foothills to the east gives the mountains their unrivaled, world-famous appearance of violently and vertically shooting up from the earth. Unique in comparison to just about any other range on the planet, no matter how many times you see them, they never cease to be stunning.

With some time to kill, I pulled up to the large visitor center near the park headquarters at Moose Junction and had a walk around inside. A beautiful, newly renovated building, it housed an impressive assortment of museum-quality exhibits on the wildlife, geology, and human history of the region, and I found myself particularly drawn to a massive three-dimensional model of the park prominently displayed near the information desk. Leaning over it intently, I slowly traced the way with my finger from the visitor center to the tiny patch of blue on the map which represented Phelps Lake.

Out at the lake tonight, Jake and I would be staying in a brand new, bright neon-yellow backcountry tent I'd purchased just before coming out West. Built to be suitable for prolonged exposure to wind and rain, it was quite the upgrade from the cheap $19.99 version I'd taken along to the Smokies. I'd deemed it necessary considering the propensity for severe weather in the Rockies, and now with a little free time on my hands, I decided it wouldn't hurt to do a bit of a test run setting it up.

Walking out the visitor center and scanning around, I found a small patch of open green grass near the back corner of the parking lot, grabbed the tent from the car, and got started. Working diligently, going back and forth between the poles and the assembly directions, it was nice to have something to keep me occupied for a bit while I waited for Jake's flight to arrive.

*     *     *

**WE TEND** to think of our national parks as idyllic, utopian wonderlands set far apart from the problems of modern society. It's all rainbows, mountains, and singing Kumbaya together by the campfire, right? While this is mostly true, it would be naïve to think that we humans don't bring along our faults and troubles with us when we go out to these incredible natural places. With over 307 *million* visitors to national parks in 2015 alone (a number almost equivalent to the total population of the United States) there is inevitably going to be petty crime, and yes, occasionally even violent crime and murder.

So who keeps us safe? Well, it's the park rangers of course. But these aren't the same park rangers who welcome you with warm, friendly smiles at the visitor center, give your child a Junior Ranger badge, and then take you out for a guided stroll along the trail somewhere. The Law Enforcement Rangers of the National Park Service are a different breed entirely. And while they may not be able to tell you where the best spots are to find moose or elk, they definitely know how to tell you when you're illegally setting up camp on public grounds.

*"Excuse me, sir,"* a booming male voice called out from behind me, prompting me to spin around wildly from fastening the rain fly to my tent.

*"Sir, what are you doing?"*

Tall, barrel chested, and absolutely ripped, the guy looked like an ex-Navy Seal behind his dark sunglasses as he exited his SUV to approach me.

"Uh, hi, officer . . . err, ranger," I replied clumsily, not knowing how to address him. "I'm just putting the rain fly on my tent. But trust me, I know there's no camping here. I'm just practicing."

"Practicing camping?" he asked skeptically. The serious look on his face made me uneasy.

"No, not practicing camping. I know how to camp," I replied back unsteadily. "I'm just practicing setting up my tent. That's all."

"Sir, if you know how to camp, then why are you practicing setting up a tent here in the middle of our parking lot?"

I started to respond, but before I could answer he interjected.

*"Sir, have you been drinking today?"*

"Drinking? God, no!" I replied back, completely taken off guard.

*"Then I need you to tell me what the hell is going on here,"* he shot back, forcefully raising his voice.

I could see the veins bulging in his neck. This guy wasn't

playing around.

"Okay, well you see . . ." I started anxiously, "I just got this brand new tent . . . I thought it would be a good idea to practice setting it up . . . my friend and I are going out to Phelps Lake tonight . . . I didn't know where else to practice . . . it's going to be my first night ever out in the backcountry . . . I just want to make sure I know what I'm doing . . ."

I stopped to gasp for breath from my incessant rambling. I'd pleaded my case like a wrongly-convicted murderer on death row.

But slowly, a subtle grin appeared on the ranger's face, which quickly turned into a wide smile. Casually, he grabbed his impenetrably black sunglasses and raised them on his forehead to look me in the eye.

"Well hell, why didn't you just say so?" he asked, suddenly laughing.

"We had three or four people go inside the visitor center and report that some guy's intoxicated out here in the parking lot trying to set up a tent for the night. I thought I was going to have to haul your ass off to the drunk tank to sober up."

I finally relaxed. Maybe I wasn't going to prison after all.

"No, no drinking today. But after running into you, I feel like I could use one . . . I thought you might tase me or something for a second there."

"Yeah, sorry about that," he replied back apologetically. "We get drunks out here all the time. If I can scare the piss out of 'em, they usually just fess up. Makes things a whole lot easier."

Climbing back in his SUV, he asked me to take down the tent when I was finished and wished me a safe stay at the lake later that evening.

"Well, I'm off to keep an eye out for some real criminals," he said, starting to pull away.

He didn't make it far before quickly tapping the brakes and leaning back out the window.

"Oh, and I almost forgot to tell you . . ." he added with an amused grin, "your rain fly's on backwards."

# 11.

**THE JACKSON** Hole Airport is one of the smallest airports in the country, so it was easy to spot Jake as he exited the plane and sauntered on into the terminal.

A tall, somewhat lanky guy with hair that is sometimes combed over, sometimes just a mess, he wore a big smile on his face as we greeted each other – partially because he was happy to see me, but mostly because he'd gotten immensely drunk on the plane ride in.

"Yeah, I was just waiting standby at the ticket counter, and out of nowhere they asked me if I wanted to take a free upgrade to first class. I said, *'heck yeah,'* that's where all the free booze are!"

Apparently, it's not enough just to get free airfare anywhere in the world.

"So, how's your big trip been so far?" he asked curiously.

I caught him up on the last few days (conveniently leaving out some of the more embarrassing parts) and filled him in on the long and laborious drive out here from Iowa. It was odd to think that while it had taken me twenty-plus hours of driving over the past two days to make it here, for Jake it had taken just a little over two and a half hours in the air from Chicago.

I briefly envied the ease of his trip, but at the same time, I have always felt that one of the reasons the West is special to me is because of the extraordinary effort it takes to get there in the first place. All of those endlessly boring and uncomfortable miles in the car serve the function of truly making places like Yellowstone and the Tetons seem set apart from the ordinary world and gives one an otherwise incomprehensible sense of just how truly remote and isolated this tucked away part of the country really is. For me, it's a case of a long journey making for a much sweeter destination in the end.

Now in the car, I briefly filled him in on our plan of action for the evening, as we hustled out to the ominously named Death Canyon Trailhead where we would begin our hike out to Phelps Lake. Turning left onto Moose-Wilson Road, widely regarded as the best stretch in the Tetons in which to spot wildlife, we distractedly peered out our windows searching for moose and bears until the unexpected, blaring horn of an oncoming RV prompted me to wildly swerve back over to my side of the road. From that point on, I let Jake do the wildlife watching.

Turning onto a narrow gravel road, the ranger from the backcountry office had told me that the two-mile path would be a bumpy ride, but this turned out to be a ridiculous understatement. An unmaintained gauntlet of deep holes, dips, and divots, it was absolutely jarring even as we crawled along at a tediously slow pace of just ten miles per hour. Convinced that the chassis of my Fusion was about to break in half, and that Jake (who was still drunk and already looking nauseous) would hurl up his guts on the dashboard at any moment, I pulled over and parked in a small turnout.

Unwilling to go any further, the two of us got out and walked the remaining mile to the trailhead. Daylight was fading fast, and now this was costing us even more time.

\*　　\*　　\*

**AFTER SPENDING** the past day and a half alone, I was immediately grateful for Jake's company, and we quickly fell into conversation as we reached the trailhead and walked along the occasionally muddy path through a forest of pine. With dusk closing in on us, we instinctively quickened our pace and were starting to really cover some ground when Jake shouted from behind me so loudly that for a moment I thought we were under attack.

*"Mooooose!"*

Quickly spinning around, my eyes followed as he pointed to the trees on the side of the trail where a large female moose casually stood scouring the ground with her enormous nose. She'd been less than ten yards away, but somehow in my hurry I'd been completely oblivious.

*"How the hell did you not see that?"* he asked.

I was at a loss. "I don't know, man. I guess I just got so focused on the trail that I forgot to keep my head up."

"Hey, no worries. As long as you don't walk by a bear, we're all good . . ."

A bear. It only further reminded me of the need to get to camp before nightfall.

Resuming the hike, we soon arrived on a high ridgeline from which we could see all the way down to the immaculate, deep dark blue expanse of Phelps Lake below. Surrounded by dense green forest, the lake was far larger than I had imagined when I'd first discovered it on my map.

With our goal in sight, but the evening becoming darker by the minute, we now set off on a blistering pace as the two of us began a race against the sun and soon found ourselves breaking out into full-body sweats from our exertion. This was probably a good thing for Jake, who looked to be sweating out most of the toxins from the flight in and now appeared to be fully recovered. In this manner, the two of us covered another mile on the steep, descending switchbacks of the trail before finally arriving at a fork in the path.

To the right: the towering, jagged walls of Death Canyon.

And to the left: the welcoming, tranquil waters of Phelps Lake.

Left, we went.

After a steep descent, we again veered on the trail and plunged into dense woods on our way for the lakeshore. Underneath the thick canopy, the world had gone nearly pitch-black and reaching into my pocket I held fast to my bear spray. With both of us nervously scanning the trees, looking and listening for threats, it was in this way we nearly tripped over the tent of another camper who'd already set up shop right on the trail. Tiptoeing around, trying our best not to disturb the person inside who was already softly snoring, we pressed on a short ways ahead until arriving at the sign for our site.

By now, virtually impossible to see, we finally dropped our packs and donned our white LED headlamps (something we should have stopped and taken the time to do twenty minutes earlier), which did much to illuminate our surroundings. Unable to locate a flat spot of ground on which to set up the tent, we imitated the camper down the path and instead opted to set up right on the trail. Quickly crossing, securing, and arching my poles in the air, I managed to erect our shelter in a matter of minutes, and was immediately grateful that I'd taken the time for a trial setup earlier that evening in the visitor center parking lot.

"Man, you're pretty slick with that tent," Jake observed, obviously impressed.

"Hey man, practice makes perfect."

\*     \*     \*

**THE FOLLOWING** morning was again spent on the trail, as we set off on a long, gorgeous loop hike around the shoreline of the lake. With nothing but time on our hands, it was a much more relaxed and leisurely affair than our hurried hike into camp had been the previous evening. Now able to stop and take it all in, we enjoyed everything the mountains had to offer, including another moose sighting and a frigidly cold swim in the lake's icy waters. It was an incredible start to the day.

Eventually making our way back to the trailhead several hours later, we returned back to Moose Junction and, after a hearty lunch, decided to set up camp down the road at the popular Jenny Lake campground where we could drive in and drop off our stuff. Our time last night and this morning in the backcountry had been great, but I suggested that perhaps this evening we do something a little bit different.

Tonight, I wanted to take Jake to my all-time favorite place in America – tonight, we were going to Jackson.

# 12.


**JACKSON, WYOMING,** is an old frontier town, but it enjoys far more prominence today than it ever did back in the days of the Wild West. Whereas most similar settlements have died away, or are still around but struggling to hang on for survival, Jackson has thrived by seizing the many opportunities afforded to it by lying in one of the most desirable pieces of real estate in all of North America – Jackson Hole.

Back in the old fur trapping days of the early 1800s, the mountain men of the era used the term *hole* to refer to a large, high valley surrounded by mountains on both sides. Thus, Jackson Hole refers to the narrow, sixty-mile long, north-south swath of land boxed in between the Tetons to the west and the lesser known Gros Ventre Range to the east. But in addition to nature lovers flocking to the national park, the area is even better known these days as a world-class skiing and mountaineering mecca for adrenaline junkies from around the globe, as well as the in-vogue vacation home destination for America's rich and famous.

Situated at the far southern edge of the valley is the town of Jackson, home to the 9,700 ordinary Wyomingites who play host to the region's many visitors. Established long ago as a small cattle outpost, the town today still has plenty of reminders of its Old West heritage but has recently emerged as something that might more aptly be labeled *Western-chic* to cater to its many wealthy visitors. In an upscale town square complete with a beautiful wooden boardwalk, those looking for the finer things in life can browse elegant galleries featuring wildlife art, posh clothing boutiques, and an astonishing number of high-end jewelry stores.

But at the same time, Jackson is also a town exceptionally welcoming to ordinary folks as well. On the same street where a vacationing CEO might go shopping and then sit down for a fine dining experience at a premium steakhouse, a regular American family can take a horse-drawn carriage ride around the square, watch reenactors perform a Wild West shootout, and afterwards find a place to grab a burger basket. In this way, the town has an uncanny ability of appealing to just about everyone.

And then there's the nightlife. And while Jackson has many establishments to delight in the company of friends, or strangers, one place in particular will always have an unforgettable place in my heart – the *Million Dollar Cowboy Bar.*

\*    \*    \*

**I FIRST** discovered the Million Dollar Cowboy Bar during my summer working in Yellowstone, after what you might call a bit of a failed romance.

Her name was Martina, a fair-skinned, dark-haired beauty from Slovakia, who had come to work out at the park that summer as part of an international exchange program. The two of us had arrived at Fishing Bridge on the exact same day, and almost instantly there'd been a spark.

Speaking with a thick Eastern European accent which brought me, and all the rest of the guys for that matter to our knees, she was the sweetest girl I'd ever met. Funny, spontaneous, gorgeous – she was perfect in every way. And somehow, against all odds, she seemed to think I was pretty great too. Together the two of us would sit with each other for meals in the employee dining room, take sightseeing trips throughout the park, and then spend our evenings watching the sunset from the beach at Yellowstone Lake. It had all the makings of a classic summer romance.

Until one day, when it all came crashing down.

The two of us had taken a trip out to see the park's famous Old Faithful geyser when, right in the middle of watching it spout its high-powered blast of steaming-hot water into the air, she leaned in close.

"This is incredible," she said, softly squeezing my arm. "My *boyfriend* back home would love this!"

*Say what?*

I had no idea how to respond. Martina had definitely never mentioned a boyfriend before. Completely shocked, I tried holding out hope that there might still be a chance for us. After all, she was here for the summer, and this guy was some 7,000 miles away. How serious could it be?

The answer – serious enough to bring my dreams of summer love crashing to the ground in a bright, fiery ball of flames. I was crushed.

It was at this point that I'd taken a recommendation from some coworkers, who told me that a night at the Million Dollar Cowboy Bar down in Jackson might be just what I needed to get back on the rebound. So, leaving the Fishing Bridge on a Friday evening after work, I'd put on my best plaid shirt and made the two-hour trip down south.

Located prominently on the western edge of the town square, a large cowboy on a bucking bronco perched high above the roof, I was initially sorely disappointed when I walked in its doors. In every way possible the place looked like a tacky tourist trap – bartenders dressed like cowboys, horse saddle bar stools, an odd display of taxidermy animals. And on top of that, it was just a bunch of dudes shooting pool and drinking beer.

*This place is a damn sausage party,* I muttered to myself. *Where the hell are all the girls?*

But that's when things started to get interesting.

Pulling up to the bar and ordering a bourbon, I sat down next to a pair of young guys in cowboy hats, who immediately took it upon themselves to strike up a conversation with me.

"How's it going partner?" the one closest to me asked.

"Uh, good . . . how about you?" I replied. I couldn't believe he had actually just called me *partner*, like we were in an old John Wayne movie.

The two of them were local ranch hands who'd driven almost sixty miles into town for the night to cut loose and celebrate the end of another busy summer work week. In fact, according to them, a lot of the guys in the bar right now were also ranchers (it turns out real cowboys actually do hang out at the *cowboy bar*). But not surprisingly, more than anything, they had actually come to chase the girls.

"What girls?" I asked, looking around the room and still coming up empty.

The two of them just looked at each other and laughed.

"Well, the dancing hasn't started yet, partner. Just hold your horses . . . they'll be here."

*     *     *

**AND SURE** enough, they were right. Because in an hour's time when the band took the stage, the women started coming in the door in droves, and the Million Dollar Cowboy Bar's small wooden dance floor was soon transformed from a vacant, empty space into a jam-packed, dizzying display of whirling, twirling motion.

Standing against the wall in the corner of the room, like the kid in high school who couldn't get a date to the prom, I watched in awe as I marveled at those out on the dance floor. The real cowboys here were *good*, and they easily stood out from the tourists in the bar like myself. Aside from their straight-fit blue jeans, no-frills cowboy hats, and scuffed leather boots, more than anything else they just carried themselves in a way that exuded a quiet confidence. From the sidelines, I watched as they approached the most attractive women in the bar, chivalrously escorted them out onto the dance floor, and then proceed to effortlessly spin them about with a seemingly endless repertoire of smooth, well-rehearsed moves. And the girls went *crazy* for it.

Feeling left out of the action, I desperately wanted to learn but had absolutely no idea what to do or where to begin. So, timidly walking out onto the dance floor, I engaged in the universally-recognized sign of lonely male desperation – *the solo dance*. Has there ever been a sight so sad and pathetic? There I was, amongst a sea of experienced dancing duos, pathetically bouncing along from side to side as I sang along. Even now, I'm embarrassed just thinking about it.

But then, feeling a touch to my arm, I turned around to see a middle-aged woman wearing a bedazzled purple Western plaid. I didn't know it at the moment, but my guardian angel had come to rescue me.

"You look lost," she said, her red-lipstick smile beaming brightly.

"Really? How could you tell?" I laughed.

"Honey, my name's Deena, and I'm about to save your sorry ass from embarrassing yourself any further, you hear? I'm going to teach you how to dance . . ."

I was thrilled and happily agreed.

"Okay, honey, so everything starts with the two-step. Surely, you've done a little two-stepping before, right?"

The dumbfounded, open-mouth expression on my face instantly told her I had no idea what she was talking about.

She smiled. "Okay, so you're a little further behind than I thought. That's alright, just follow me . . ."

I grabbed her two hands to get started, but she immediately

laughed and pulled away, as if she'd never seen anything so ridiculous in her life.

*"Where the hell are you from, boy? That's not how you hold a woman . . . this isn't the junior high mother-son dance!"*

Aggressively taking my right hand, she now sensually placed it on the small of her back. *"This* is how you hold a woman." I could already feel the nervous beads of sweat running down my forehead.

"Now, the two-step . . ." she continued.

At first, she started off in the lead while I clumsily followed. And although it took a few stumbles and stepping on her toes in the beginning, remarkably, I quickly got the hang of it. Soon, we reversed roles, and in short order I was leading her.

"Look at you, you're a natural!" she said encouragingly, as I felt my confidence start to rise.

Now it was time for some spins, and much to my surprise, I again quickly caught on. Soon I had a repertoire of three or four basic moves, which in no time at all had me feeling like a smooth operator . . . not as good as the veteran cowboys, but still good enough to fit right in.

Our lesson complete, Deena gave me an enormous hug to celebrate. My cheeks hurt from smiling so much.

"Honey, there's nothing left for me to teach you! Now you just have to go and ask some girl your *own age* to dance with you."

With my characteristic sheepishness, I replied, "Well, that's *if* she says 'yes' . . ."

*Whack!*

Out of nowhere, Deena had unexpectedly smacked me on the side of the head. Hard.

*"Oww! What the hell was that for?"*

"I don't want to hear any of that attitude, mister!" she said reprimanding me, her finger pointed in my face. I recoiled back, afraid she might hit me again.

"You're my star student . . . of course she'll say 'yes!' Now go!" she said, as she literally pushed me into a crowd of attractive girls who were standing nearby.

\*   \*   \*

**AND JUST** like that, a tradition was born. In that first night alone, I must have danced and chatted with more single girls than I ever had in my life . . . all because I could dance. Previously the guy on the sidelines, now thanks to Deena, for the first time in my life I was a hot commodity. It was incredible.

And so it was, every Friday night for the rest of the summer, I would make the two-hour drive down to Jackson to swing dance at the cowboy bar until last call. Never able to afford the notoriously expensive lodging in town, I'd usually end up staying the night in the front seat of my car in a dark, tucked away corner of the town's welcome center parking lot. Upon waking up on Saturday morning, I'd often times drive back up to Fishing Bridge, shower up, change clothes, and come back to do it all over again later that night. Having infinitely more luck with the girls in Jackson than I ever had with the ones up at Yellowstone, those trips down to the cowboy bar each and every weekend still stand out as some of my favorite moments from that wonderful summer.

And now, as Jake and I walked down the boardwalk two

years later, I reveled in all of the familiar sights and sounds and the memories they carried with them. We parked in the same welcome center parking lot where I used to fall asleep at night. We had dinner at my favorite Mexican restaurant in town, Merry Piglets Cantina. And of course, we ventured into the Million Dollar Cowboy Bar, where I'd spent so many wonderful evenings drunkenly dancing the night away.

And in the same way a certain song on the radio can take you back to a specific time in your life and allow you to vividly recall how you felt in that moment, such was the feeling now as the band took the stage and an eclectic crowd of cowboys and tourists set the bar awhirl in motion. Magically, it triggered in me an old, familiar sense of excitement and anticipation that will always uniquely belong to this small wooden dance floor in Jackson, Wyoming. And even though it was a pretty tame night in comparison to the old days (like a couple of old men we left the bar by ten o'clock), sometimes in life there is nothing better than revisiting a place from your past and simply taking the time to reminisce.

\*  \*  \*

**THE ALARM** went off at 5:30 a.m., and still half-asleep, I struggled to find it and hit the snooze. With Jake already having to fly back home, his early morning flight to Chicago made for a rough start to the day. Emerging outside the tent, I thought perhaps I was still dreaming as I found myself staring upon an enormous bull elk with large pointed antlers meandering through the campground just yards away from our site. With no one else awake at this early hour, we were the only ones to witness as he casually proceeded by and continued to graze just inches away from the tents of other unsuspecting campers who continued soundly sleeping inside.

Eventually, after wishing Jake a fond farewell at the airport terminal, I drove directly back to the campground to sleep for another few hours before starting the morning. Today was going to be different, and I was going to need all the rest I could get.

Heading back up to Yellowstone, I was about to embark on the solo-phase of my journey and camp in the backcountry for the first time on my own.

It was finally time to test my mettle out in the wilderness and find out what I was made of.

# 13.

"HELLO!" SAID the friendly female ranger as I walked into the backcountry office at the Bridge Bay Ranger Station a few miles south of Fishing Bridge. "Here to pick up a permit?"

Informing her that I was, she directed me to a table along the far wall with a stack of white binders containing maps and information on Yellowstone's designated backcountry campsites. Immediately, I began rummaging through the contents of the binder labeled *Canyon*.

While certainly not as large as its big brother in Arizona, the Grand Canyon of the Yellowstone is, nonetheless, a spectacular natural wonder. Stretching on for 20 long miles, this enormous, deep chasm in the earth is home to the fast-moving waters of the Yellowstone River as it carves its way through immense, thousand-foot cliffs on both sides. For most visitors, it's best known as the home to the often-photographed Lower Falls, where the river surges off the edge of a spectacular 300-foot drop on its way to a dazzling freefall below. One of the most visited sites in the park, the area is perpetually busy and swarming with tourists.

But as the old saying goes, "99 percent of visitors to Yellowstone see just 1 percent of the park." And while many popular places like the canyon can be insanely crowded and chaotic, most of these same locations can feel absolutely desolate if you take the time to get away from the parking lots and head just a half mile or so onto a trail.

With this in mind, I rummaged through the maps in the binder at the backcountry office and discovered a little-used trail capable of transporting one deep into the heart of the canyon and far away from the sightseers. Known as "Seven Mile Hole" due to its distance from Lower Falls, the trail proceeds along the high ridgeline of the canyon before dropping deep down to several primitive backcountry campsites right along the banks of the Yellowstone. It is the only trail in the park that goes all the way down to the bottom of the canyon, and consequently, it was exactly where I wanted to go.

Obtaining my permit, I got back in the car and headed north towards my destination, eventually entering the enormous grassland known as the Hayden Valley. Frequented by visitors and lined with roadside pullouts for those wishing to exit their vehicles and survey the landscape, the Hayden Valley is regarded as one of the premier places to view wildlife in all of Yellowstone. Often teeming with enormous herds of bison, visitors with their spotting scopes can also be treated to views of grizzlies, elk, wolves, otters, and virtually every other wild creature that calls the park home.

Enthralled by so much wildlife and lured by such an incredible setting on which to gaze upon them, passers-through tend to take their time, and sometimes it can be downright painful for someone who's in a hurry. Indeed, traffic this day was at a snail's crawl for much of the drive, resembling rush hour on the freeway of any major American city. Slowly moving along, I tried to be patient and took the opportunity to take in the views myself – they are beautiful, so long as you keep your eyes on the valley and not the bumper-to-bumper traffic in front of you.

Eventually though, still continuing north, I exited the valley and minutes later was skirting the rim of the canyon. Driving two miles or so past the incredible drop at Lower Falls, I parked and got out of the car next to an enormous glacial boulder which marked the beginning of the trail to Seven Mile Hole.

# 14.

**I USED** to read a lot of spy novels when I was younger and watch movies like *Jason Bourne* and *James Bond* with complete fascination. They lived such exciting, action-packed lives, with every daring exploit inevitably followed by something even more death-defying the next time around. But the more you read about the accounts of real-world covert agents, the more you discover that the seemingly glorious world of espionage is, in actuality, "long periods of boredom, punctuated by moments of sheer terror," to quote the oft-used saying. In other words, it's not all that it's cracked up to be in the movies.

It turns out the same is also true of solo-hiking and camping – it appears gloriously adventurous and heroically independent on the outside, but in reality it's just a lot of walking around, talking to yourself, and sleeping on the ground. To slightly modify the previous saying, camping out in the woods by yourself is really just "long periods of boredom, punctuated by a few *small victories* along the way."

It wasn't that the hike into Seven Mile Hole was particularly difficult. In fact, it was actually fairly easy for the first four and a half miles as I followed a pleasantly maintained trail along mostly flat terrain. But the further along the trail remained flat, the more it became unavoidable that the last mile was going to be *incredibly steep*. From my high vantage on rim of the canyon, the mighty Yellowstone River looked nothing more than a tiny, sea-green ribbon and felt impossibly far below.

Of course, getting down wasn't the hard part. Sure, the terrain was dusty and gravelly, requiring careful footing, but even the winding switchbacks and couple of severely sharp descents were manageable. What scared the hell out of me was fast-forwarding in time to imagine how unbearable this same slope was going to be tomorrow on the way *up*. This was a serious grade, more than 1,000 feet in just a little over a mile.

Eventually making the long descent to the bottom, I finally arrived at my campsite, which was situated on a wide shelf of the canyon wall and perched high above a 100-foot, vertical drop-off to the teeming, white-capped current of the river below. Assembling the tent roughly three feet from the brink of the cliff, from a seated position inside I could enjoy a totally unobstructed view of the water as it rushed through this secluded, almost never-seen section of the canyon. Using a small fallen tree as a natural guardrail, I prayed it would be enough to prevent a strong gust of wind from sweeping the tent (along with me inside) off the edge and into oblivion.

\*     \*     \*

**BEARS HAVE** an almost supernatural ability to smell things. A grizzly, for instance, has a sense of smell roughly seven times stronger than that of a bloodhound and thousands of times stronger than that of a human. In fact, they are quite adept at sniffing out and tracking down food from *miles* away. Compare this with most people, who can't even smell the pizza burning in the oven, and it's a pretty impressive feat.

It's for this reason that the park service in Yellowstone requires all backcountry campers to hang their scented items, such as food and garbage, high off the ground and at least 100 yards from their tent sites. In this way, it is far less likely that a pleasant trip in the woods will be interrupted in the middle of the night by a 700-pound visitor trying to claw his way in for a snack. The slang for this is "hanging a bear bag" and with the rope work and knot-tying that goes into it, it kind of makes you feel like you're back in Boy Scouts all over again. Or in my case, for the first time.

Back in the Tetons, the park service had provided a bear-proof storage unit at our campsite, so this was my first go at hanging my food. Not possessing a separate bag for the purpose, after dinner I instead went about loading all of my remaining food and other scented materials such as tooth paste, deodorant, and bug spray into the green nylon sack normally used to carry my sleeping bag. Going through all my supplies and then double-checking again, it was important not to overlook anything which might give off even the slightest hint of a smell or fragrance. The bottom of the canyon wasn't prime bear territory, but there was no sense in taking any chances.

Tying the bag to a long string of rope, I left a sizeable ball of cord at the end and, cocking back my arm, heaved it up and over the tall crossbar apparatus the park service had constructed here. Much to my delight, the small ball of rope elegantly sailed over the high beam and fell silently back to the ground near my feet. Marveling at the simple pulley system I'd created, I proudly hoisted the sack high into the air as if it were Old Glory on the flagpole.

With the bag now elevated, I coiled the remaining cord around the thick, sturdy trunk of a fallen tree and quadruple-knotted it to ensure it would hold in place throughout the night. Feeling confident that everything was in ship-shape, I stepped back proudly to evaluate my handiwork. And while admittedly it wasn't a complicated task, there was still an undeniable sense of satisfaction looking up at the bag as it hang high above in the air. For a complete novice, I had done pretty well.

*Small victory.*

\*　　\*　　\*

**I AWOKE** the next morning to discover that I had indeed not been blown off the edge of the cliff in the middle of the night. Another *small victory.*

Now, already terribly warm and stuffy in the tent, I quickly climbed out into the fresh morning air and slipped on my boots to head down to the river banks. Walking through faint clouds of steam, I passed small bubbling hot springs emanating from the rocky ground – subtle reminders of Yellowstone's immense supervolcano which lie just below the surface.

The Yellowstone supervolcano, an immense magma chamber underneath the park believed to contain enough molten lava to fill fourteen Grand Canyons, gets a lot of publicity. Seemingly every year, there's speculation that a catastrophic eruption capable of wiping out the entire United States is imminent. In reality, the National Park Service says an eruption in the next 1,000 or even 10,000 years is highly unlikely. Still, if we do happen to be around when it blows (experts who study it place the odds at roughly 1 in 730,000 annually) there is little question the results could be devastating.

At the time, however, I wasn't much concerned with supervolcanos and was instead much more preoccupied with quenching my morning thirst. Dipping my filter bottle into the river, I greedily drank the cold water much too quickly and still feeling parched immediately went back for more. In no time at all, I was overcome with an intense splitting headache, the same kind you'd get as a kid when you ravenously attempted to eat your ice cream too fast. Unfortunately, this was only mild discomfort compared to the pain that lie ahead on the mercilessly grueling climb out of the canyon.

I'm sure I could muster up some elegant prose to describe the torture that was climbing more than 1,000 feet in just over a mile, but suffice it to say, it absolutely kicked my ass. The work was hot, straining, exhausting, and all of that was just within the first ten minutes. The going was mind-numbingly slow under the weight of my pack, and slopes that had taken only minutes to descend on the way down now took as much as a half hour on the way up.

It was discouraging to think of the time and punishing effort going into such marginal gains. In the steepest sections of the climb, progress was literally only inches at a time, and I stopped to rest often, sometimes only ten or fifteen yards from where I'd just rested before. Sweating profusely, salt stinging my eyes, I baked under the intense rays of the sun and greedily drank water to replace the fluids I was rapidly losing.

It took forever, but somehow, I eventually reached the top. Of course, from here this meant there were still four and a half miles to go before reaching the trailhead, and what had been a leisurely hike just the day before was now almost completely unbearable. Overcome with exhaustion by the time I finally reached the car, I hastily kicked my boots to the floorboard, lie motionless in the driver's seat, and feebly turned the air conditioner on to full-blast. It was the last thing I remember before falling off into a deep, dreamless sleep.

*Major victory.*

# 15.

**AWAKENING IN** the car sometime later, I got back on the road and began making the hour-and-a-half drive towards my next overnight camp located in the far northeastern corner of the park. Leaving behind the canyon, the road climbed steadily in elevation as it approached the base of popular Mount Washburn, home to one of the park's last remaining fire lookouts. Here, visitors willing to make the strenuous day-hike to the summit can be treated to an unrivaled view of Yellowstone in all directions and on a clear day see all the way south to the Tetons. Originally, it had been my intention to make the climb, but that was before Seven Mile Hole. Now, the thought of just going up a small flight of stairs seemed daunting.

Bypassing the mountain and continuing on, I soon

approached the Tower-Roosevelt Junction where the main road splits in two – left to the park headquarters at Mammoth Springs, or right to Yellowstone's little used, remote Northeast Entrance. It was here that I spotted a small sign for the Roosevelt Lodge, my last chance to get a hot meal and supplies before heading out into the middle of nowhere. With stomach rumbling, I pulled onto a long gravel path and headed towards the outpost.

A modest, rectangular cabin with two small stone chimneys rising from the ends, perhaps a dozen visitors lazily reclined out front in the large wooden rocking chairs that adorned the lodge's long, shaded front porch.

A sign near the front steps of the building proudly proclaimed:

*ROOSEVELT LODGE*
*Established in 1906 in commemoration of a camping*
*trip to this region by President Theodore Roosevelt*
*accompanied by naturalist John Burroughs, April, 1903 . . .*

For me this was pretty exciting, considering I have what you might call a bit of a historical "man-crush" for Theodore Roosevelt.

Who graduates from Harvard at the top of their class and then leaves behind an up-and-coming career as a New York statesman to follow their dream of becoming a *cowboy* in North Dakota? Well, Theodore Roosevelt, of course.

Leaving it all behind and impulsively taking a train across the country to the Badlands, overnight Roosevelt became a rancher raising cattle, mending fences, and even serving as a deputy sheriff who spent his time famously chasing down horse thieves. This wasn't "dude ranching," this was the real deal. Spending several years on and off at his cabin on the banks of the Little Missouri River, it was about as far away from the life of an affluent New Yorker as one could possibly get. So transformative was the experience, he would later write in his memoirs that he "never would have been President if it had not been for my experiences in North Dakota."

Speaking of the Presidency, it was here that Roosevelt almost singlehandedly rescued America's early national parks from complete ruin.

Almost thirty years before he took office, when Yellowstone became the world's first national park in 1872, it had actually been a bit of sad joke. Without the appropriate manpower or funds from the federal government to maintain the rule of law, the park was instead overrun by poachers, timber-cutters, squatters, and others who aimed to profit off the land. In effect, it had become a den for crooks and thieves. By the time Roosevelt took the Presidency in 1901, Yellowstone's survival, along with America's four other national parks at the time, was very much in doubt.

But rather than throwing in the towel on the newly conceived idea of national parks, Roosevelt instead doubled-down on them. By creating five more national parks during his presidency, he reaffirmed the government's commitment to protecting America's great places, and along with forests, wildlife reserves, and national monuments, set aside nearly 230 million acres of land during his two terms in office (unbelievably, this equates to an area of land roughly the size of Texas, Florida, and South Carolina combined). For this, history would later come to know him as *The Conservation President.*

Incredibly, all of this would only go on to become a small part of Roosevelt's legacy. In addition to his life as a cowboy and United State President, the man would also:

- Author 45 books
- Write over 1,000 magazine articles
- Be widely considered one of the foremost wildlife experts of his era
- Earn the Medal of Honor for acts of valor and bravery in the Spanish-American War
- Win the Nobel Peace Prize
- Establish the National Collegiate Athletic Association (you're welcome college football and March Madness fans)

Hell, even after retiring, Roosevelt was a badass. Several years after leaving the White House, he literally became an *explorer* leading a small team of men on a dangerous expedition into the heart of the Amazon jungle to chart the previously unexplored *Rio da Duvida* (River of Doubt).

Needless to say, Teddy was a pretty remarkable guy. And now as I sit down for lunch in the Roosevelt Lodge, I took an odd sense of pride in knowing that I was exploring this same tucked away section of Yellowstone that he himself had trekked through a little over a hundred years before. For all I knew, my hero could have made his campfire on this very spot where I now sat eating my bacon cheeseburger and French fries.

# 16.

**AFTER MY** lunch at the Roosevelt Lodge, I resolved to call Kellie back at home and let her know I had indeed survived my first night alone out in the wild. But with my cell phone still displaying the same "No Service" message it had since all the way back at the Dunraven Pass near Mt. Washburn, I was at a bit of a loss.

While much of Yellowstone has recently picked up service, here in the northeast section of the park there are still thankfully no cell towers. Thus, I'd decided to continue another twenty miles or so down the road to the gateway town of Cooke City, a few miles outside the park, where I was sure I'd be able to pick up a signal.

Situated in a narrow valley where the jagged Absaroka and Beartooth mountain ranges meet, Cooke City is a sleepy outpost located just across the Wyoming border in the Treasure State of Montana. Driving into town, I barely had time to blink before I again found myself reentering the forest . . . the tiny community of just over 140 year-round residents now entirely in my rearview mirror. Slowing down and cranking the wheel, I pulled a sharp U-turn and made my way back, this time parking the car and getting out to stretch my legs and have a look around.

With only one narrow street and not a single traffic light, Cooke City still feels like an old frontier settlement lined with small hotels, restaurants, shops, and drinking establishments that are still affectionately referred to as *saloons*. This early in the summer, still before the main tourist season, there were only a handful of other visitors on the main strip which was remarkably quiet and still. Set against a pristine snowcapped mountain backdrop, I couldn't help but feel as if I'd stumbled upon a wonderful hidden gem of a community.

It's hard to imagine that under different circumstances, tiny Cooke City might have been one of the largest boomtowns the West has ever seen. Famously known as the New World Mining District to those in the business, the region began attracting miners in the late-1800s for the massive treasure trove of gold, silver, and copper deposits being discovered here in the mountains.

But surrounded by towering peaks on one end, and Yellowstone National Park on the other, it proved nearly impossible for these early prospectors to profitably transport this immense mineral wealth to outside markets where it could all be sold. For this, railroad access was needed – but the mountains proved too costly and difficult to build through, and the new national park was off limits to lay down tracks. Thus, the railroad never came to Cooke City, and by the 1920s most of the miners had left town for better opportunities elsewhere. Today, the land is set aside for conservation by the federal government, and surveys of the region show that millions upon millions of dollars of precious metals continue to lie dormant up in the mountains.

So in spite of the massive riches surrounding it, Cooke City continues to remain a small, unassuming mountain community. And in the same way the railroad never arrived, neither did the cell towers. Reaching for my phone to call Kellie, I was again greeted with the now familiar "No Service" message and instead sauntered into the local gas station to inquire about a payphone. I was directed to the Soda Butte Lodge next door, which from the sounds of it may have been the only place in town to make an outbound call. It was strange being in a community so disconnected from the outside world, but at the same time it was also kind of amazing. Here it actually seemed possible to get away from the worries and distractions of our modern lives, which I tend to think is the main reason people choose to come out to places like Montana and Wyoming in the first place.

I honestly couldn't remember the last time I'd used a payphone, but I'm pretty sure it was back in junior high when my friends and I would go into town to the local Pizza Hut and dial random 1-800 sex-line numbers and talk to whichever sultry sounding women answered on the other end of the line. (Sadly, this is what passed for entertainment in the small town of Colona, Illinois, where I grew up.) Nowadays though, I couldn't even recall seeing a payphone anywhere, and it was a fun novelty inserting my spare change into the slot and putting the bulky receiver up to my ear as I dialed out on the antique contraption.

"Hello?"

"Hey, dear. It's me!" I said excitedly to Kellie on the other end of the line.

"Oh, hey!" she said, happy to hear from her long-lost significant other. "I didn't recognize the number, where are you calling from?"

"I'm in Cooke City, Montana. Can you believe I'm calling from a *payphone?*"

It was great to hear her voice, and as we happily exchanged stories from our day, she informed me that she was currently stuck in backed-up traffic near the local shopping mall back home. I couldn't help but laugh. From where I sat in Cooke City, in the middle of the lonely Absaroka-Beartooth wilderness, the two of us might as well have been on completely different planets.

# 17.

**HAVING MADE** my call, I left Cook City and reentered the park on the way to my evening's destination — the famous Lamar Valley of Yellowstone. Such is the abundance and diversity of wildlife in this forty square-miles along the Lamar River that it is often referred to as the Serengeti of North America. Indeed, as I entered the valley, many hundreds of bison could be seen out in lush grasslands lazily grazing and resting. But somewhere out there, currently out of sight, was another more frightening resident of this vast expanse.

Although the last remaining wolf pack was killed in Yellowstone in 1926 under predator extermination policies of the day, wolves were eventually reintroduced into the park in 1995 by biologists who were interested to see if the species had what it took to make a comeback. In an experiment in conservation that garnered worldwide attention, fourteen gray wolves were transported from western Canada down to Yellowstone, where in the middle of January people lined the roads to watch as they passed through the northern gates of the park via horse trailer. Broken off into three small packs and released with tracking collars into the Lamar Valley, biologists everywhere now watched and waited, as they held their breaths to see what would happen next.

As it turns out, the experiment worked better than anyone could have ever imagined. The original packs immediately thrived in their new ecosystem, taking advantage of drastically overpopulated elk herds, who had previously experienced few natural predators. Soon, the wolves started making happy, healthy little wolf pups, and the rest is history. Now, over twenty years later, they have spread throughout the park and around 100 wolves in ten separate packs call Yellowstone home, while many hundreds more populate the surrounding region.

As I pulled my car over to the side of the road, parking at an overlook by the trailhead, it was early evening and still about two hours from dusk when the wolves of Lamar would start to come out and become most active. Already though, in excited anticipation, were dozens of wildlife watchers lined up along the railing of the overlook, their powerful binoculars and scopes trained out to the valley, slowly scanning from side to side searching for any signs of movement.

Why would I choose the epicenter of wolf activity in Yellowstone to stay the night, especially after my nerve-racking encounter with the *I-thought-was-a-wolf* coyote just days earlier? Well, I suppose I figured this time around there weren't likely to be any face-to-face showdowns. Wolves are famously shy of humans and, in spite of their bad rap, in the entire documented history of North America there have only been *two* confirmed fatal attacks of a human by a wild wolf – neither occurring in the Lower 48. Unless someone had been feeding them by the side of the road like they had the coyote (which I seriously doubted) there was little chance of any up close and personal run-ins. This evening, I was just hopeful for the opportunity to view from afar and maybe get some good pictures I could show my friends back home.

Getting out of the car to examine my pack, I double-checked that I had all of the essential supplies I would need to spend the night in camp. Satisfied that everything was in order, I wrestled the hulking bag onto my back, slipping my arms through the straps, and was immediately buried by its overbearing weight once again. My quads ached heavily and my back was sore, still feeling the effects of the painful climb out of the canyon earlier that morning. Fortunately, tonight would be a cake-walk in comparison – a short three-and-a-half-mile jaunt over relatively flat terrain to a place along the Cache Creek, which downstream flows into the Lamar River.

Ready to head out any minute now, I spread my large foldout trail map over the hood of the car and verified the route I was to take on my way out to the campsite. But in the midst of my final preparations, I was startled by a collective gasp from the crowd on the overlook, which caused me to raise my eyes out towards the valley.

Off in the distance, two small blurs raced from left to right, easily several hundred yards away and well out of range of my farsighted eyes. Fumbling about frantically for my binoculars, I finally managed to pull them out of my pack but was now unable to find the speeding blurs in my lenses. Continuing to scan about wildly, at last, they appeared in my sights.

What I saw was amazing – a lone, grayish-white wolf locked in a full-out, maniacal pursuit of a pronghorn antelope that was literally running for its very life. The two of them were absolutely *flying*.

Not surprisingly, the pronghorn had used its superior quickness (at an incredible 55 mph, they're the second-fastest mammal on Earth) to open a distance of perhaps fifteen yards in front, but the wolf was relentless . . . desperate even. Against all odds, he seemed to inexplicably be closing down the gap as the two of them continued to race across the valley at almost unfathomable speeds – I had never seen living things move so fast in my entire life.

From our vantage on the overlook, it felt like a movie playing out before our eyes, but in my mind I tried to imagine what the very real, life-and-death struggle must be like up close – the sound of frantic hooves pounding against the ground, grass thrashing, dust flying, the wolf snarling with determination, saliva flying from his mouth as he raced to close the gap.

Frantically he kept the chase, continuing to inch closer, as the two of them raced over a small ridgeline in the distance and disappeared from sight. And just like that, it was over. The valley was once again perfectly still, as if the whole thing had only been a dream.

\*     \*     \*

**WHILE INCREDIBLE** to witness, the chase had proved to be quite unnerving as well. Sure, I had come out to Lamar because I wanted to see the wolves, and deep down I knew they posed no real threat. But it's easy to be brave when you're daydreaming from the safety and security of your living room, watching a PBS Nature documentary on the couch while munching on a bag of microwave popcorn. It's quite another thing to be brave when you're actually standing on the edge of that immense, lonely valley and know that once you step foot out there, you're entirely on your own. Now it was very real, and suddenly, it was quite frightening.

My first instinct was to turn around and leave immediately. The Pebble Creek Campground was just a few miles up the road back towards the Northeast Entrance. Surely, there I could find a nice little spot for the night, surrounded by the comfort and security of other fellow travelers. Heck, I could even go back to Cooke City and grab a nice dinner while I was at it.

But I quickly dispelled the thought from my head. If I had wanted comfort and security, I could have just stayed back home in Iowa. The whole point of this solo-phase of the journey was to test my mettle and push my limits. And there was no better way to do it than by facing my fears – wolves or no wolves, I was going out to that valley.

Allowing several minutes to pass, time which I spent gathering my courage, I took a deep breath as I folded my trail map and began descending down from the overlook. Walking through the crowd, I incurred a variety of confused looks and strange glances as I passed. I attempted to appear confident, trying not to betray the fact that I was shaken by what I'd just witnessed.

I began my journey tentatively, but the further I walked from the road, the more my feelings of uneasiness grew into something more. Soon the people and their vehicles at the overlook became smaller and smaller, until eventually they were just specks in the distance. With each step I took, the more vulnerable I felt. Quickly, I was consumed with fear and began wildly scanning my surroundings, looking for any signs of the wolves I knew to be out here. And while I couldn't see them, I was suddenly quite sure that somewhere out there, they were most certainly watching me.

Now pulling out the long machete I hauled in my pack for emergencies, I grasped it tightly in my right hand while simultaneously clutching my bear spray in the left. Nervously proceeding through the valley, I slowly climbed the same ridgeline where the wolf and pronghorn had raced over just twenty minutes before and fully expected to see the wolf eagerly waiting for me on the other side.

Now fully hidden from view of the tourists back at the road, I was completely and utterly alone, and my nerves began to play tricks on me – I'd freeze at the slightest sound of the wind rustling the grass, peer over my shoulder to make sure I wasn't being followed, and somehow convince myself that far-off shapes in the distance were predators, though inevitably they were just rocks or fallen trees. Short of breath and with sweaty palms, I was suddenly overcome with a lightheadedness that gave the whole ordeal an almost hallucinatory feel.

Fighting the urge to turn and run back to the safety of

civilization, I continued along in this primal, fear-stricken state for well over an hour, until finally arriving at the banks of Cache Creek. It had been the longest, most miserable three and a half miles of my life.

\*     \*     \*

**THE CAMPSITE** was set in a small collection of trees in an otherwise empty, soggy meadow, perhaps fifty yards from the gravelly banks of the creek. Because of my frequent stops to investigate imagined threats, and an overly-cautious pace which had served to prolong my agony, the hike in had taken far longer than it should have.

It was at this point that I started to question what the hell I was doing out here. I'd set out on this hike trying to prove how brave I was, but had instead spent most of the time double-fisting a can of bear spray and a machete like some madman escaped from an insane asylum. I was dirty, I stunk, I was lonely, I was scared – and for what?

Fortunately, the ritual of making camp and setting up my tent did much to calm my nerves and put me at ease. What's more, this was the first backcountry site I'd been at all trip where I was finally permitted to establish a campfire. In many places out West the risk of man-made wildfire is simply too great for campfires to be allowed when staying out in the wilderness. But apparently, here at Cache Creek, the risk was sufficiently tolerable for the park service to allow it.

Gathering the driest small twigs and sticks I could find, I arranged them in a small teepee formation around the handful of newspapers I'd brought along as kindling and watched with excitement as they quickly ignited. Soon, with the addition of larger pieces, my humble pile had unexpectedly morphed into a roaring backwoods bonfire. Celebrating my own private Tom Hanks *Castaway* moment, I didn't go quite so far as to tear off my shirt and start dancing around the flames screaming *"I've made fire!"*, but I did experience a brief surge of manly pride, nonetheless. I was still far from being a backwoodsman, but it felt good to at least be making progress.

My reward for all of this was a bag of large, extra puffy marshmallows I'd purchased earlier in the day at the Roosevelt Lodge for just this moment. After my tense and stressful evening on the trail, I was now grateful to have a delicious, sugary treat to make it all go away. Sharpening the end of a long narrow branch, I skewered two of them and patiently hovered them near the glowing orange embers of the fire until they were perfectly crisp and golden brown, careful not to get them too close lest they spontaneously burst into flames. At first, I worried the sweet aroma might attract any nearby bears, but ended up ignoring the risks and rationalized this might actually be a good thing. A few bears might help to keep the wolves away.

Biting into the gooey, molten-sugar center, I felt the weight of my stressful evening fall from my shoulders. Making a second batch, I enjoyed this simple pleasure by the campfire as I watched a long and grueling day turn to dusk. Enjoying the warmth of the fire until it gave out, I poured some water over top of it, hung my bear bag, and eventually shuffled back to the tent where I was immediately overcome with a crushing fatigue. The physical exhaustion from my morning climb out of the canyon, along with the intense emotional drain from my hike in the valley this evening, had finally caught up with me, and my body and mind were demanding a reset.

Quickly drifting off to the low, soothing roar of the creek, I was out cold before the sun had even fully set in the sky.

\*     \*     \*

**WAKING UP** the next morning, I was shocked to realize I had somehow managed to sleep for over half a day – thirteen hours.

Stepping out of the tent and feeling the cool mid-morning breeze, I was instantly amazed at how completely refreshed and revitalized I felt in comparison to the night before. Sticking to my usual routine of fetching water, eating a light breakfast, and tearing down camp, I began making my way back along the trail and had a remarkable bounce in my step and mental clarity that I hadn't felt in days.

Already past ten o'clock in the morning, it was much easier to stride comfortably along the path than it had been the previous evening. Right now, the wolves of the Lamar Valley were likely to be fast asleep after a long night and early morning of hunting, and I felt completely safe as I made my way north back towards the car. Taking out my camera and snapping as many shots as possible, I made an effort to appreciate the beauty of Lamar in a way I hadn't done the night before – a ground squirrel poking his head out along the trail, a patch of blue wildflowers, a purple butterfly in flight, a pair of pronghorns on a hillside. It's amazing the difference a good night's sleep can make.

Arriving back at the trailhead, I was renewed with

excitement for the journey ahead. There was still so much I wanted to do and see, and with a rested and refreshed mindset, I was more eager than ever to continue.

But at the same time, I also knew it was time for a change. I'd tried convincing myself that I was up for one more night in the backcountry, that I wanted to push my limits and test myself, but deep down what I really wanted was a *break*. I'd spent the last two nights by myself in the wilderness, and truth be told, I was starting to feel a bit lonely. The thought of another evening alone seemed depressing at this point, and what I really wanted more than anything was to go into town somewhere, relax, and have a good time.

Fortunately, I knew just where to go.

# Part 3

# Wyoming Backroads

# 18.

**LOCATED AN** hour from Yellowstone's East Entrance, the town of Cody is a small community of just over 10,000 residents. However, back when I worked at Fishing Bridge, the town had very much been "the big city" for us civilization-starved youngsters, who were all more than happy to make the 80-mile drive to enjoy its simple amenities such as a movie theater, fast food, and a SuperWalmart. Thus, perhaps it's no wonder I once again found myself leaving Yellowstone and making my way through an arid, rocky canyon landscape on the way to Cody.

Named in honor of the legendary Wild West showman of the late 1800s, William "Buffalo Bill" Cody, the town sits just minutes away from the Buffalo Bill Reservoir and the Buffalo Bill Dam, which in turn sit adjacent to Buffalo Bill State Park.

(Are you sensing a theme?) Currently driving past the dam, I now entered a long, cave-like tunnel blasted into the base of Rattlesnake Mountain, an enormous rock colossus which borders Cody on its far western edge. Entering the mountain via a narrow, dimly lit half-mile passage resembling a journey through the center of the earth, I soon emerged on the other side and caught sight of the town on the near horizon.

My destination was the historic Irma Hotel, located right on the main strip of Sheridan Avenue in the heart of Cody's vibrant downtown. Built by Buffalo Bill himself in 1902, and named for his daughter, the building is terrifically preserved and is still in fact a fully-operational hotel where guests can spend the night in the same rooms used over a century before by iconic Old West figures like Annie Oakley, Calamity Jane, and of course Buffalo Bill himself. Even the attached restaurant has remained much as it was in the olden days, happily serving up sliced and fried Rocky Mountain Oysters (bison testicles) for guests' culinary delight.

I'd originally intended to grab a drink at the hotel's downstairs saloon and enjoy the evening kicking up my feet on the shaded outdoor porch, but apparently everyone else in Cody had the same idea as well. Scouting things out, there wasn't a single seat to be had, and I didn't feel like standing on my weary legs a second longer than I had to.

Instead, I made my way across the street and down the block where I heard the soft sound of an acoustic guitar emanating from the outdoor patio at the Silver Dollar Bar. Eating their dinners and sipping their drinks from an array of picnic tables, a small crowd was listening to the song of a lone cowboy singer playing in front of them. In his early forties, with a hand-painted sign that announced his name, Steve Frame had made the three-and-a-half-hour drive from Casper, Wyoming, to perform for the evening.

I instantly took a liking to Steve. He's the kind of guy who uses the term *honkytonk* as a verb – as in, "Come on y'all, let's honkytonk!" And while I'm not a huge fan of country music, it's not exactly country music that he plays – it's country western. What's the difference? Well, think less trucks, break-ups, and drinking . . . and more horses, love ballads, and ranching.

Either way, regardless of the genre, I couldn't help but tap my toes and sing along to some of his more lively tunes, as Steve himself was having such a great time playing them – a happy, wide smile beaming from his face the entire time. But then, like every good performer, he could also flip that switch and take you somewhere emotional as well. At one point he brought up another local musician from the audience, a middle-aged man who looked like a diesel mechanic with greasy hair under a camouflage trucker's cap, and together the two of them sang a duet of *Amarillo by Morning* that was so beautiful, I swear it almost made my eyes water. They were seriously that good.

But above all else, Steve Frame was a showman. With endless enthusiasm, homespun humor, and a folksy cowboy charm, he was arguably at his best in between songs when he took the opportunity to get to know the audience.

"Excuse me there, ma'am. How are you? Would you mind telling this wonderful crowd of folks where you're joining us from tonight?"

The almost exclusively tourist crowd was from all over the

123

map, but no matter what far flung corner of the country they'd come from, Steve had a quick one-liner for all of them. For the retired couple from Bangor, Maine, he had a corny lobster joke. For the vacationing family from Coeur d'Alene, Idaho, he had a corny joke about potatoes. And for myself from Davenport, Iowa, he had a corny joke about . . . well, corn. Okay, come to think of it, all of Steve's jokes that night were what you might term "dad jokes," but somehow he always managed to pull them off in a way that left everyone in the audience laughing wildly. With Steve Frame, corny was cool.

I was having such a great time that I was actually planning on staying at the Silver Dollar for the remainder of the evening when Steve introduced an old Garth Brooks hit titled *Good Ride Cowboy*. A boot-stomping rodeo song, written about a real-life Wyoming bronco riding champion, Steve performed a rip-roaring rendition that absolutely brought down the house.

*. . . when that whistle blows*
*and that crowd explodes*
*and them pickup men are at your side*
*they tell you good ride cowboy . . . good ride!*

And suddenly, I had an idea.

\*     \*     \*

**CODY, WYOMING:** *RODEO CAPITAL OF THE WORLD* read the large block letters fixed atop the grandstand at the Stampede Park stadium on the outskirts of town.

Officially designated the state sport in 2003 (yes, a handful of states actually have an official sport . . . Alaska's is dog mushing, for instance) rodeo is a veritable religion in Wyoming, and Cody is its holiest city. Inspired by Steve's lively rendition, I'd hurriedly gulped down the remainder of my drink and sped over to catch the unique summer tradition known as the Cody Nite Rodeo – an event dating back to before World War II, and the only nightly rodeo left in America.

Behind the outdoor arena, the fading sun created a dark silhouette of the rolling hills, and rose-tinted clouds mixed with a blue sky to create one of the most impossibly beautiful sunsets I have ever seen. It was the perfect Wyoming evening.

Already a half-hour late, the action was in full force by the time I bought my ticket and made my way into the arena. Immediately, I was hit with sensory overload. Like the county fair, the smells of hotdogs, nachos, and fried food wafted through the air, mixing with the subtle, but ever-present aroma of horse manure emanating from the arena below. Music blaring from the loudspeakers, brilliantly lit stadium lights shining down, an emcee giving a rapid-fire play-by-play, and a couple thousand roaring fans – it was a head-banging rock and roll show, only with farm animals.

Walking in, I'd just caught the tail end of one cowboy's frenzied ride on a maniacal bronco that tossed him so high in the air that I couldn't help but cringe as he came plummeting back down to earth. This, of course, only made the crowd erupt even more wildly, and the DJ in turn responded by blasting the music even louder. This thing was crazy, nothing like what I'd expected.

And so it was I spent the remainder of the evening watching this wild spectacle play out before me, as cowboys and cowgirls competed in an array of competitions from bareback bronco riding, calf roping, team roping, and barrel racing (don't worry, I had no idea what any of these terms meant beforehand either).

And then there was the halftime entertainment, an event known as the "calf scramble," where the children of the audience were invited down to try their hand at chasing down two young calves with bright blue ribbons attached to their tails. This night though, the two young cows were running circles around the nearly one-hundred young humans. Frantically sprinting from one end of the arena to the other, they easily outmaneuver the children who repeatedly gave chase and wildly launched themselves through the air trying to grab the ribbon, face-planted in the dirt, and then got up to do it all over again. By the time it was all said and done, a few of the kids were crying, a handful were gasping for their inhalers, and all of them were hopelessly dirty and defeated as they exhaustedly stumbled out of the arena to the awaiting arms of their parents. In most places, this type of event would be a child-endangerment lawsuit just waiting to happen, but thankfully here in Wyoming it's still considered just good ole' fashioned fun. I hadn't laughed so hard the entire trip.

Staying until the very end, I departed with the rest of the crowd and turned west out of town back towards the Buffalo Bill Reservoir where I set up camp for the night along the shores of the lake. Listening as a cool, steady breeze brought waves crashing ashore, followed by the light pitter-patter of rain on the roof of my tent, I reflected on the evening. My night in Cody hadn't been an adventurous and rugged affair spent out in the backcountry . . . but damn if it wasn't a whole lot more *fun*.

\*     \*     \*

**AWAKENING ON** the shores of the reservoir the following morning, I'd gotten up early while the rest of the campground was still quietly sleeping and drove to the town McDonald's. Here I sat comfortably in my booth snacking on a hashbrown and Egg McMuffin, while the sizeable old-folks breakfast crowd drank their morning coffees. Huddled closely together, they talked about the Cody Cubs high school baseball team and had an in-depth discussion about the ten-day weather forecast. My mind was elsewhere though. Today was going to be a long day on the road.

It was time to start slowly making my way south for Denver, Colorado, where tomorrow afternoon I would be joining up with a longtime friend of mine, Chris, for the last leg of my journey. And while I was excited to hit Rocky Mountain National Park for a couple of days, most of all I was just looking forward to finally having some familiar, friendly company again.

But I still had one more solitary day to go. And with 500 miles of desolate Wyoming highway ahead of me, I left Cody to see what I might find along the way.

# 19.

**OUTSIDE OF** Yellowstone and the Tetons, much of the rest of Wyoming is like the surface of the moon. Barren, rugged, chalky, dry, colorless – if it weren't for the sagebrush and occasional fence posts along the road, looking out the window one might very easily think they were an astronaut on an Apollo lunar mission.

But situated along the banks of the Bighorn River in central Wyoming, the isolated community of Thermopolis (population 3,000) is a welcome oasis. A bit of a ways off the beaten path, it doesn't garner much attention and at first glance appears much like any other quaint and charming small Wyoming town. But obviously there's something different going on here. I mean, what's with a name like *Thermopolis*, right?

Well, as it turns out, the name is aptly descriptive –

combining the words *thermo* (hot) and *polis* (city), Thermopolis is indeed Wyoming's *hot city*, as it is rather unassumingly home to the largest mineral hot springs on the entire planet.

For this reason, I was ecstatic to discover that my route towards Colorado would take me right through the town and nearby Hot Springs State Park. A sacred site to the Shoshone and Arapahoe Indians, who believed the area to be home to ancient spirits, the hot springs have long been thought to have healing powers for those who enter them. Accordingly, visitors to the park are encouraged to bring not just their cameras, but their swimsuits as well. Needless to say, after six consecutive days of hiking and nights spent sleeping on the ground, the idea of a little hot-tub action was pretty appealing to me at this point.

I'm not sure why, but I guess I had imagined soaking in the springs in some secluded, tucked away spot in the wilderness. Wading into a natural pool carved into the earth, watching the water bubble forth before my eyes – I'd envisioned something remote and pristine. But, alas, Hot Springs State Park isn't exactly what you'd call a wilderness experience. At 135 scalding degrees Fahrenheit when it emerges from the ground, the spring water is far too hot for visitors and is instead pumped into three different swimming facilities on the park grounds where it is allowed to slightly cool.

Two of these venues are commercial waterparks complete with slides, high-dives, and the throngs of screaming children that naturally gravitate to these sorts of things. The third facility, however, the Wyoming State Bath House, is where all the old people go to get away from them. This was right up my alley.

Interestingly, the bath house is actually the fulfillment of a 120-year-old treaty between the U.S. government and the Shoshone and Arapahoe. With the hot springs once located in the northeast corner of the Shoshone Reservation (now the Wind River Reservation) which encompassed both tribes, they agreed to sign over the land and hot springs to the federal government on one strict, non-negotiable condition – that a portion of the springs be set aside for public enjoyment, free of charge . . . forever. Thus, while the two waterpark facilities charge admission, to this day the Wyoming State Bath House remains completely free to the public.

Emerging from the locker room in my swim trunks, towel slung over my shoulder, I walked out to the deck of the modest outdoor pool and was immediately struck with the color of the water. A cloudy, pastel shade of blue, it was unlike anything I had ever seen before. In the background lie the beautiful white-terraced rock formation of the spring itself, which fed the pool from underground.

Wading in, I sighed with relief as I sank in up to my neck and let the wonderful warmth start going to work on my aching body. Lounging in the water with my sunglasses on, I looked like a vacationing honeymooner in Cancun instead of a lone traveler driving through a remote stretch of Wyoming. It was a terrific change of pace.

With the place all to myself for the moment, I enjoyed the peace and quiet for perhaps ten minutes before an older man in his mid-to-late seventies appeared from the building. With snowy white hair and ghostly-pale skin to match, he could have easily been mistaken for one of the Indian spirits believed to inhabit the hot springs as he slowly walked towards the pool.

Stepping into the water, I smiled and nodded my head as he waded past.

The next few minutes passed by much as they had before, quietly relaxing with my eyes closed. But soon, rather unexplainably, I began to feel a strong urge to talk with the man who'd just walked into the pool with me. At first, I couldn't figure out why. What would the two of us possibly talk about?

But then it hit me – an unsettling realization. I hadn't had a real, face-to-face conversation with someone since dropping Jake off at the Jackson Hole Airport *three days ago*.

Sure, there had been a few transactional pleasantries exchanged with some cashiers at various points along the way, but those hardly counted much as meaningful human interactions. I was starting to become a recluse, and I needed to talk with someone fast.

"Water sure is nice, isn't it?" I called out to him.

"Huh?" he replied back loudly. "What did you say?"

He was hard of hearing. I should have figured.

*"WATER SURE IS NICE, ISN'T IT?"* I shouted back again.

"Oh yeah, real nice!" he called back smiling.

And thus began a pleasant conversation in the middle of the pool with a friendly stranger named Bill. He and his wife were currently in the middle of a long, scenic road trip through the West and had been on the road for nearly three weeks now. They were finally in the process of heading back home to Seattle, Washington, and their next stop was to visit Yellowstone tomorrow.

"Yeah, I've been happily married to the same beautiful

woman for over fifty years," he said beaming with pride. "We still like to go on our adventures."

As a soon-to-be newlywed, I was blown away and took the opportunity to ask if he had any words of advice.

"Sure, I guess if I had to pick one thing, it would be pretty simple: just always make sure to put her needs before your own. If you can do that, you'll have a happy marriage."

*That's it?* I thought. *This guy's been happily married for half a century and the best piece of advice he can give me is some lame cliché?* I wasn't letting him get off the hook that easy.

"Anything else?" I asked, looking for more.

Now he really put his head down and seemed to be mulling it over. Finally, after a long silence, he lifted his eyes and said, "Well, I guess it's also kind of important to know when to leave each other the hell alone, too."

Okay, now this was interesting.

"What do you mean?" I asked curiously.

"Well, take our road trip for example. It's been great, and I'd definitely do it again. But by this point, we're really starting to get on each other's nerves a little bit. Three weeks stuck together in a car can be a little tough, you know?"

"So how do you know when it's time to give each other space?"

"Oh, trust me, you'll know," he chuckled. "Women can be pretty emotional sometimes. Generally, when she starts raising her voice, I know it's time to leave her be for a little bit."

"That makes sense," I replied. "You can't have a fight if you walk away before it starts."

"Well, it's not quite that easy either," he responded. "Sometimes when she raises her voice, it means she really wants you to stay and talk it out with her. You have to be able to know the difference."

"And how do you know the difference?"

"Oh, I don't know," he said laughing heartily. "Fifty years of experience, I guess . . ."

I shook my head. Marriage was going to be complicated.

\*     \*     \*

**BEFORE RESUMING** the road south for Colorado, I opted for a short detour north of Thermopolis to the tiny, sparsely populated community of Kirby, Wyoming, just twelve miles away. Home to only 92 residents and set amongst a treeless landscape on a dry, grassy plain, it still very much has the feeling of a remote pioneer outpost somewhere on the frontier. With only a handful of pickup trucks, not a single person to be seen, and a small smattering of old homes and buildings, you may be wondering why I, or anyone else for that matter, would ever drive out of their way to come here.

But nestled alongside the easy moving waters of the Bighorn, it's here that the Wyoming Whiskey distillery pumps out its big, beautiful barrels of small batch bourbon. Having tried it for the first time a couple years back at the Million Dollar Cowboy Bar, it was my beverage of choice that summer while swinging around the dance floor in Jackson and has remained a favorite of mine ever since – a little taste of Wyoming in every drop. Having been so close by, I had come for a tour of the distillery, but most importantly, let's face it, for the free drinks at the end. (Yes, leave it to me to drive out to the middle of nowhere just to get my hands on some free booze.)

Driving through Kirby, which took all of about ten seconds, I arrived at the distillery's small welcome center where I narrowly missed out on the two o'clock tour by just a few minutes. Spending the better part of the next hour meandering around the gift shop, passing the time looking at merchandise and browsing through coffee-table books, I waited for the day's final tour to begin at three. The time passed slowly, but right on time, a friendly young lady walked out to greet me.

"Welcome to Wyoming Whiskey!" she said warmly, her eyes scanning the rest of the room only to find it empty. "Did the rest of your group go outside already?"

But there was no one else. It's not like people flock to Kirby, Wyoming, at three o'clock on a Wednesday afternoon.

"Actually, I think it's just the two of us," I informed her as we walked out the door.

I was about to learn the hard way that this type of thing is not meant to be a solo activity. Think about any similar tour you've ever been on. You hang around the back of the group, talking with whomever it is you came with, while the guide up front takes everyone around announcing random facts along the way. At the end, when it's all said and done, you get your free drinks, and everyone leaves having had a great time.

But when you go by yourself . . . that's when things start to get weird.

In my case, the afternoon basically ended up resembling a bad first date between me and my tour guide. It started with the strange, painful awkward silences in between stops on the tour. Sure, we attempted to fill the voids in conversation with mindless small talk, but the fact of the matter was the two of us had absolutely nothing in common and the potential topics of conversation had dried up quickly. And then there was the chemistry – that was off too. Hell, the two of us actually ran into each other and bumped heads one time when I went to hold the door open for her because she was the girl, and she went to hold it open for me because she was the tour guide. It was all incredibly confusing.

On top of this, like every first date, I felt an intense need to pretend to be super interested in everything she had to say. Thus, as she explained the fermentation process, distilling process, and a whole bunch of other scientific processes I didn't actually understand (yet was too embarrassed to let on) I found myself inexplicably "ooohing" and "aaahing" as if I were utterly fascinated for some reason. Didn't she know I was just there to drink at the end?

Don't get me wrong, she was very nice. But the thing was going terribly. By the time we finished touring the rick house, the warehouse-style building where the whiskey is aged, I was definitely ready for the tasting to begin.

"Well, are you ready to head back to the . . ."

*"Yes!"* I blurted out reflexively.

She laughed out loud, equally as relieved as I was for the whole ordeal to finally be over. A few minutes later, when the two of us arrived back at the welcome center, she briefly disappeared into the backroom before emerging with my drink in hand.

"Here you go," she said cheerily. "Enjoy!"

After driving out to the middle of nowhere and putting in nearly two hours of my time to get this drink, you can imagine the letdown I felt when she handed over a tiny plastic shot glass, three-quarters of the way empty, with an imperceptibly tiny sliver of amber brown whiskey at the bottom. It was as if she'd measured the thing out using a few squeezes of an eyedropper.

Forcing a fake smile, trying to hide my disappointment, I took it and put the diminutive cup up to my nose. Swirling around the few sad drops of whiskey inside, I attempted to say something intelligent to show her I'd been listening on the tour.

"Ah, I can really smell some of those notes you were talking about earlier," I said. "I'm going to have to really take my time and savor this."

Considering there wasn't even half a sip in the cup, it was arguably the most ridiculous thing a person has ever said.

Looking confused, she politely smiled and walked away, surely wondering to herself what the hell I was talking about. With her back turned, I swallowed the meager contents of the cup and hastily retreated for the exit.

On the scale of bad first dates, this one topped them all. At least this time there wouldn't be the demoralizing *"sorry, I'm just not that into you"* text the next day.

\*     \*     \*

**FROM HERE** I rejoined the highway and resumed the road down to Colorado, passing through the imposing, vertical rock walls of the Wind River Canyon just south of Thermopolis. If much of the rest of Wyoming is like being on the moon, then this 11-mile stretch of road along the banks of the Wind River is like stepping back into *prehistoric times*.

137

With some of the oldest rock formations on the planet, over 2.9 billion years old, it's easy to get the feeling driving through that you've in fact gone back to an age when dinosaurs ruled the Earth. Fittingly, the area today is a hotbed of fossil excavation activity. Once home to large numbers of enormous, long-neck herbivore dinosaurs who are continuously being discovered here, recently the unearthing of an extremely rare *Allosaurus* (the only-slightly-smaller cousin of the legendary predator *Tyrannosaurus Rex*) has set the worldwide paleontological community ablaze with excitement. For a former dinosaur-lover like myself, who watched Jurassic Park on repeat as a child (stopping only to rewind it in the also now-extinct VCR), it was a fun place to let my imagination run wild for a bit.

But alas, snapping back to the modern world, I soon left the canyon and completed the two-hour drive to the city of Casper where I took in dinner and a late movie before continuing another several hours along the dark, lonely interstate for the state capital of Cheyenne. Here, barely able to keep my eyes open, I pulled into a crowded hotel parking lot just ten miles north of the Colorado border. The dimly-lit green numbers on the car's radio console read *1:18* in the morning.

Leaving the engine on for heat and softening the volume of the radio, I reclined back and was soon, once again, passed out to the world for another night spent in the front seat of my car. Tomorrow, I would bid a fond farewell to Wyoming and complete the short drive to Chris's apartment in the Denver suburbs, where for the first time in days, I looked forward to a hot shower, a home-cooked meal, and maybe even an air mattress to sleep on the following night.

# Part 4

# Rocky Mountain National Park

# 20.

**A DAY** and a half later, after spending the previous afternoon and evening relaxing at his apartment in the Denver suburbs, I stood with Chris as we made a final double-check of our gear before making the 100-mile drive to Colorado's famed Rocky Mountain National Park.

Chris and I go way back. Having known each other since we started playing travel soccer together as kids, back in high school I'd spent so much time at his house that his mother, Jan, had aptly labeled me her "other son." With me already being out West, I'd been happy to make the drive down to Colorado to rope him into my little adventure.

"Got your rental boots?" I asked sarcastically.

(Earlier that afternoon, Chris had spent far more time asking about the return policy on the boots he was buying than he actually did contemplating the merits of the footwear itself. *"So, just to be clear . . . if I wear these for the weekend and they don't feel good, I can still return them, right? No matter how scuffed up, dirty, and broken in they are?"* he'd asked two separate associates at Cabela's.)

"Yeah, I got my boots," he shot back defensively.

"Hey, I'm not trying to pull one over on anyone," he added. "I just don't know if I'm going to like this whole hiking and camping thing . . . I don't want to be stuck with a $150 pair of boots if I'm never going to wear them again."

You have to realize, Chris isn't exactly what you'd call the *outdoors type*. Rather, he's the guy who was voted "best dressed" in our high school graduating class and had a walk-in closet full of American Eagle button-down shirts and faded jeans. The experience of roughing it out in the wilderness was going to be completely new for him. His wife, Christina, had secretly told me the night before that he'd been nervous about the trip for weeks now.

"Promise me, you and Nick will look out for him?" she'd asked with concern.

Nick, Christina's brother, was the third member of our group that weekend. A former college track star, football player, and now competitive body builder in his free time, not only are he and Chris brothers-in-law, but they also happen to be old college roommates. Consequently, the two of them share the unique male bond that can only be forged by living in filth with someone, drinking copious amounts of alcohol with them out of a beer bong, and then turning around and marrying the guy's sister. I'd met Nick several times before, most recently at Chris's wedding the previous summer, and he'd been an absolute riot. Living just a half hour up the road, also outside of Denver, we'd agreed to pick him up on our way out to the park.

\*     \*     \*

**BEGINNING THE** roughly two-hour drive from the city, the three of us wound our way northwest beneath snow-covered peaks as we steadily climbed into the noticeably thinner air of Colorado's Front Range. With Chris's car in the shop, I'd volunteered to drive the Fusion and at times feared the worst as the engine revved inordinately loudly and struggled mightily during the steepest portions of the ascent – I didn't even want to imagine what it would cost to get a tow truck out here. But soon cresting the halfway point at the Berthoud Pass, where a sign near the side of the road announced an official elevation of 11,307 feet, we had already reached twice as high as the Mile High City of Denver. From here, it was now a gentle downward coast to the park's tiny southern gateway community of Grand Lake, which itself lie an impressive 8,300 feet above sea level.

Imagine a quaint, quiet beach town somewhere on the East Coast. Waves crashing ashore, children playing in the sand, seagulls gliding in the air . . . and then drop it in the middle of the Rocky Mountains. That's Grand Lake. Nestled against steep, jutting peaks on one side and idyllic, pristine lakeshores on the other, this tucked-away settlement of 460 individuals on the southwestern edge of the national park may very well be the most perfect small town in America.

Not only is the town's namesake lake the largest natural lake in Colorado, but it also rather unassumingly serves as the headwaters for the lifeline of the American Southwest, the mighty Colorado River. Here at Grand Lake, the river's 1,500-mile journey originates with enormous amounts of mountain snowmelt from the park before running down through southeastern Utah, transforming into treacherous rapids in the Grand Canyon of Arizona, being converted into electricity at the Hoover Dam in Nevada, and ultimately ending as a trickle in the turquoise, hammerhead shark-infested waters of the Gulf of California off Mexico's Baja Peninsula.

As we arrived late that afternoon, the lake couldn't have looked more beautiful as a light summer breeze carried a small gathering of white sailboats out across the water. Picking up our camping permits at the Kawuneeche Visitor Center, we now made our way downtown to a local outfitter to rent our mandatory bear-proof food canisters (an act which seemed to deeply trouble Chris), before taking a leisurely stroll down the main boulevard looking for one last hearty meal.

The town was busy, but not crowded, and walking by a few happy vacationing families and couples we sauntered past mom and pop burger joints, pizza parlors, ice cream shops, and confectionaries, before eventually being drawn to an appealing Mexican restaurant with a chalkboard sign out front advertising "Two for One" happy hour margaritas.

Taking our seats at a large open booth, we were soon being served our drinks and taking large gulps while we chatted and awaited our dinner. I was about to learn, however, that Chris wasn't the only one nervous about heading into the woods that evening. Nick had his reservations, too. Although his were of an entirely different nature.

"So," said Nick, chomping down loudly on a tortilla chip before continuing his thought, "what made us possibly think this would be a good idea . . . drinking margaritas and then eating a crap-ton of Mexican food before going out into the woods for two nights?"

He was just getting started.

"I mean, so what do we do if we gotta . . . you know . . . take a *dump*? Do we just pop a squat and let'er rip?"

I could already tell this was going to be a lovely dinner conversation.

"No, man," I responded. "Well . . . actually, sort of. I mean, you gotta dig a hole in the ground first and then bury it."

"Bury it? Like a fucking cat?"

Yep, just like a cat, I told him. This in turn led to more questions.

"So what do we dig the holes with . . . our hands? And then what do we wipe with . . . a pine cone, or something?"

I briefly cringed at the thought but assured Nick that I'd come fully prepared – a mobile bathroom steward if you will. Not only did I have a spade in my pack for digging, I had plenty of toilet paper, and I'd even brought along some hand sanitizer so we could wash up afterwards.

This seemed to calm him down, at least until Chris opened his mouth.

"But you know, Nick, we have to carry out our toilet paper after we use it," Chris shot in. "We can't litter in a national park."

Nick looked bewildered, eyes wide as they flashed from Chris to me. "*WHAT?*" he shot back. "Tell me he's joking, Rob. There's no way I'm carrying out my own *shitty* toilet paper, am I?"

But he wasn't joking. When the park service says, "Leave No Trace," they mean it in the most literal way possible. We were indeed going to be packing everything out with us.

"If it makes you feel any better, I brought Ziploc bags . . ." I said trying to comfort him.

# 21.

**AFTER DINNER,** it took only a matter of minutes to drive to the nearby Tonahutu Trailhead just north of town. By this time it was already early evening, and after a couple of margaritas back at the restaurant, we were all feeling pretty good as we parked the car in the small gravel lot and unloaded our gear. It felt strangely comforting to once again strap on my heavy pack and prepare for another trek out into the woods. It had only been three days since I'd hiked out of the Lamar Valley in Yellowstone, but having detached myself from the wilderness recently, it already seemed as if it had been weeks. The guys were equally excited as well, and lugging their own packs onto their shoulders, we finally set out on the Tonahutu Trail and began our march towards our evening campsite three miles north.

It was invigorating to be back on the trail, and immediately I felt an added spring in my step that was surely the result of the past few days of rest. From the get-go, it was a gradual, but persistent uphill climb, as we followed the strong, crashing current of the Tonahutu Creek through dense tree cover away from Grand Lake and into the interior of the park.

I'd taken the lead to start and had set a brisk pace, but early on I could tell the guys were struggling. Nick is a gym rat, and Chris is a former athlete himself, but neither of them were quite prepared for the unique challenge that is trudging uphill for several miles under the weight of a forty-pound pack. I remembered my own first time vividly – the first mile's a piece of cake, the second mile your legs start to feel heavy, and the third mile . . . well, that's when your legs turn to pure lead, and your pack suddenly feels as if there are a couple of sandbags stashed away inside.

Two miles in, with them already starting to fall behind, I decided it would be wise to rest for a few minutes before they fully reached the sandbag stage.

*"Man, are you trying to kill us, Rob?"* Nick asked, huffing and puffing for breath as we reached the top of a small hill. He let his pack slip off his shoulders and go crashing to ground. "You're like a damn puma or something out here."

"Yeah," said Chris, finishing a long drink from his water bottle, "or like a mountain lion."

Nick and I paused to look at each other.

"Did you just say a *mountain lion?*" Nick shot back incredulously.

"Yeah, why?"

"Dude, you know a puma and a mountain lion are the *exact*

same thing, right?"

"No, they're not!" Chris fired back defensively. He immediately turned towards me, the so-called animal expert, to back him up on the matter.

"Sorry, man. They're the same . . ."

Looking embarrassed, he attempted to brush it off. "Yeah, well . . . whatever. All I know is that Rob was absolutely flying. You think we can slow it down a bit or something? *Damn . . .*"

I apologized and confessed that perhaps I'd gotten a bit carried away. (Sure, I'd been trying to show off a little as well, but I wasn't going to tell them that.) Either way, I suggested that perhaps Chris take the lead, and we could all follow him at a more leisurely and relaxed pace until we arrived at camp.

Soon lugging our packs back on, we were once again on the move.

"Chris, you watch out for the mountain lions up there. We'll keep an eye out for the pumas," Nick shouted from the back.

\*    \*    \*

**IF CHRIS** and Nick thought this was a rough hike, I can't even imagine what they would have thought of the original trek I had planned for us.

Initially, a month earlier when I first began planning our route, I'd spent several days of intense research attempting to find an itinerary for the absolute perfect Rocky Mountain adventure. I was looking for something memorable, something exciting. Finally, after much deliberation, I had it – a spectacular 30-mile loop taking us high over the Continental

Divide through some of the most incredibly rugged and awe-inspiring backcountry in the park. This was unquestionably the badass kind of adventure the three of us would talk about for the rest of our lives. Picking up the phone and excitedly dialing out to the park, I was eager to log my itinerary with the rangers and reserve our campsites.

But my bubble was quickly burst. On the other end of the line, the ranger who answered the phone at the backcountry office informed me, in not so many words, that rather than creating the ultimate Rocky Mountain adventure like I thought, I had instead spent the past few days crafting the ultimate Rocky Mountain death trap.

*"Uh . . . yeah . . ."* said the ranger speaking hesitantly, as if trying to find a way to put it delicately. "Have you actually been out here to the park before, sir?"

Nope.

"Okay, are you a professional or highly-seasoned climber?"

Not at all.

"Well, don't get me wrong," he said politely, "the trip you just laid out sounds absolutely amazing . . . maybe in September. But are you aware of just how dangerous it could be up there above the tree line in early June?"

He continued, "When you guys are looking at going up to the pass at the Continental Divide, the whole area is still going to be completely snowbound. I'm not trying to tell you what to do or anything, but unless everyone in your party is experienced in alpine climbing and comfortable with crampons, ice axes, et cetera, I would strongly urge you to reconsider."

I swallowed hard. I could already see the headlines:

*AMATEUR HIKERS FOUND FROSTBITTEN*
*AND STARVING IN ROCKY MOUNTAINS*
*GROUP LEADER BLAMED FOR LACK OF PLANNING*

Obviously, this wasn't going to work. Fighting back my embarrassment, I informed him that perhaps it would be best if I looked for something a little bit different.

Luckily, he was more than happy to help me plan another route more suited towards our abilities. Almost immediately, he recommended the Tonahutu Trail and a pleasant-sounding campsite named *Paintbrush* situated a few miles north of Grand Lake. After the epic adventure I'd originally envisioned, a place called "Paintbrush" seemed a little tame for my liking, but the ranger was adamant we would absolutely love it. Not only was it perhaps the best location in the entire park to spot wildlife, but according to him, it was also one of the most beautifully scenic as well.

"Trust me, you won't be disappointed," he said confidently. "And most importantly, you're not likely to die trying to get there."

\*    \*    \*

**ARRIVING ROUGHLY** an hour before sunset, Paintbrush was located on the other side of the Tonahutu Creek on the edge of a large grassy meadow aptly, if uncreatively, named *Big Meadows* on our map. Perhaps it would have been more accurately labeled *Big Swamp*. As a result of fresh rainfall and recent snowmelt, the entire area was in fact one enormous marsh, with several inches of standing water lurking in most places below the tall grass.

The main problem with this was the mosquitos. While we hadn't encountered a single bug on the way there, as the sun began to set, these hellacious, pestering little vampires emerged in full force. Lathering ourselves up with a highly concentrated, and probably unhealthy dose of DEET bug spray, it had all proved futile as we were soon forced to retreat for the night into the cramped quarters of our three-person tent.

"Rob, are you sure you stashed those bear canisters far enough away from camp?" Chris asked uneasily, as the three of us switched off our headlamps and lie down for bed.

"Yeah, of course I did. Why?"

"Well, obviously I don't want a freakin' grizzly bear busting in here tonight . . . is that so crazy of me?" he shot back.

"Calm down, man," I replied. "First of all, there aren't any grizzly bears in Colorado. And second, there are only like twenty black bears in the entire 400-and-something square miles of the park. We're more likely to run into a *Bigfoot* out here than we are a bear."

But even if the bears didn't get us, there were still the violent criminals in the woods to worry about as well.

On the way out to Paintbrush, not more than a quarter mile away, we'd run into a sketchy-looking man illegally camped along the trail. For reasons we couldn't fully explain, the guy had totally creeped us out. Maybe it was the way he'd hurriedly zipped a large black duffel bag and defensively stood over it as we approached him to chat, or the way he refused to explain why he wasn't at a registered campsite. Or perhaps it had something to do with the three separate occasions he'd nervously asked whether or not we'd seen any park rangers out on the trail that evening. Either way, he'd sufficiently put us on edge.

"So, I've been thinking . . ." said Nick, "what if he's *cartel?*"

It wasn't a totally crazy thought. Ever since Colorado legalized marijuana back in 2014, federal authorities had warned about the influx of Cuban, Columbian, and Mexican drug cartels moving into the state to grow their product and then ship it elsewhere throughout the U.S. on the black market. It wasn't a secret. Everyone in Colorado knew they were there.

"Those fuckers are crazy," Nick added. "I've seen *Breaking Bad.* If that guy's cartel, he might just come here in the middle of the night and murder us to eliminate us as witnesses."

We all laughed, mostly to hide our nerves. Of course he was joking, but still . . .

"Well, on the plus side," said Chris, "at least we're all in here together. I mean, strength in numbers, right?"

We all thought about it for a few seconds.

"Yeah," replied Nick, "or it just makes it easier for him to take us all out at once."

And on that cheerful note, the three of us proceeded to lie in the dark in an eerie, uncomfortable silence – Nick and I on the ends, Chris wedged snuggly in the middle. Between hungry black bears and cartel hitmen, there were plenty of things to be afraid of that went bump in the night in Rocky Mountain National Park.

# 22.

**I AWOKE** in the middle of the night cold and shivering, and pawed around in the dark to find my winter jacket and stocking cap, which I promptly put on and slid back into my sleeping bag. I'd purchased this particular sleeping bag, rated for -20 degrees Fahrenheit, specifically for these two nights in the Rocky Mountains where I knew the high elevations could lead to some chilly nighttime temperatures. Needless to say, I wasn't thrilled by the fact that it couldn't even keep me warm on a night that only dipped into the low 40s. But now bundled up in the same outerwear I would have worn to go skiing, I managed to fall back asleep and rest soundly for the remainder of the night.

Rising the next morning, I stumbled out of the tent in my thick winter attire and casually strolled away from the campsite to the edge of the meadow while Chris and Nick continued to sleep. Bathed in warm rays of morning sunlight, the sharp nighttime chill had already vanished, and I discarded my jacket as I quietly reflect on the fact that today marked the last day of my journey through the West.

It brought with it a mixed bag of emotions. On the one hand, much of me felt relieved – it felt like a long time since I'd seen Kellie, a long time since I'd slept in my own bed, and in many ways I couldn't help but feel that I'd accomplished everything I'd set out to do on this incredible adventure. On the other hand, a part of me never wanted to leave.

With Chris and Nick soon making their way outside the tent amongst a chorus of their own early-morning yawns, we put on our boots to go refill our empty water bottles at the Tonahutu Creek.

Ambling out into Big Meadows, we hopscotched our way on scattered grass clumps, using them like small stepping stones to bound our way across the endlessly green expanse without walking in the ankle-high standing water below.

Arriving at the creek and unscrewing the lid of my filter bottle, I dipped it down into the crystal clear waters of the stream which shown all the way through to its muddy brown bottom. Taking my first sip, the frigid chill was a shock to my nervous system and did more to jolt me awake than any strong, caffeinated cup of morning coffee ever could.

Chris and Nick, on the other hand, weren't so fortunate to be able to enjoy the same immediate gratification of a morning drink like I was. The two of them had brought along old-fashioned iodine to purify their water, and instead of instantly sipping, they were forced to drop in a few tablets and spend the next thirty minutes vigorously shaking their bottles as if making a martini. It's a huge pain in the ass, especially when you're thirsty.

"Cheers, guys!" I said, holding up my bottle and taking another hearty swig. I purposely embellished it with a long, overdrawn *"aaahhhhhh"* at the end.

Nick just glared at me as he set his watch for a half hour and started shaking, while Chris raised his non-shaking hand and flipped me the middle finger. We were having such a wonderful time bonding.

It was moments later that we spotted a large moose casually feeding near the far tree line on the opposite side of the meadow. Continuing to scan our surroundings, we quickly sighted another grouping of at least a half dozen more. Curiously staring at us, these ones were much closer, perhaps just forty yards away on the other side of the creek. We'd been so focused on hopping around the meadow trying to keep our boots dry, and then gathering water, that we hadn't even noticed them.

Sensing that we'd now taken an interest in them, one member of the herd, a particularly burly-looking bull with incredible antlers, parted ways from the group and began slowly making his way towards us.

*"Um, guys . . ."* Chris stammered nervously, *"do you think we're too close?"*

It was a fair question. In places with high moose populations, it is a well-known fact that more people are injured every year by moose than by predatory animals such as wolves, mountain lions, or bears. It's not that moose are inherently aggressive, but people seem to simply forget their manners around these large animals and encroach far too brazenly into their personal space. They mistakenly believe that since moose appear sluggishly docile and don't have sharp teeth or claws, they must be safe.

But like just about anything that's 6-7 feet tall at the shoulder and weighs 1,000 pounds, moose can indeed be very dangerous if provoked. If you don't believe me, just ask a fifty-year-old Colorado woman who a little over a year earlier, in nearby Gilpin County, got too close to one outside her subdivision. Displeased with the situation, the moose in turn charged, rammed her over, and then proceeded to *stomp on the woman repeatedly*. Four broken ribs, fifteen stitches later, and with staples in the back of her head, she was eventually released from the hospital.

But from where we stood, a respectable distance away on the other side of the creek, I assured Chris that we would indeed escape with our lives. Sure enough, the rogue moose took only a few steps further before again nonchalantly burying his head back in the grass. The rest of the group soon followed suit, as they had apparently lost interest in us as well.

\*     \*     \*

**TEARING DOWN** camp and hiking back to the main Tonahutu Trail after breakfast, it was impossible not to stop and admire the little slice of mountain paradise we currently found ourselves in. With the creek meandering through the grassy meadow, and several snowcapped peaks off in the distance reaching up to the clouds in a perfectly blue sky, it was like standing in the middle of a postcard. (Ultimately, the snapshot I took that morning would become the cover for this book.)

But it was time to leave, and initially proceeding north, we continued to skirt the meadow for another mile or so before plunging into dense timber as we veered eastward towards our next campsite at Lower Granite Falls. Arriving just before lunchtime, it came as a bit of a surprise that, in spite of the name, there was actually no waterfall to be found here. In fact, compared with Paintbrush and Big Meadows, this new spot was a major letdown. Tucked deep in the woods under a canopy of trees, it was dark, dreary, and offered nothing in the way of the expansive mountain vistas we'd enjoyed earlier that morning.

Knowing the mountains had more to offer, the three of us quickly decided there was only one thing left to do after lunch – press on even further.

## 23.

**WE'D FIRST** heard of Haynach Lake the day before from a spry-looking senior citizen who'd been standing behind us in line at the Kawuneeche backcountry office. In spite of his white hair and dark oversized sunglasses typically reserved for the elderly, he had the lean, chiseled body of a man half his age. Overhearing us discuss our travel itinerary with the ranger, he'd leaned in curiously.

"Say, you boys wouldn't happen to be going up to Haynach Lake while you're out that way, would you?"

The three of us looked at each other, not knowing how to respond.

"Uh, I'm not sure," Nick finally replied for all of us. "I guess we don't really know anything about it."

"Well, in that case, you fellas should really think about

163

going to check it out. It's pretty high up in the mountains, just a shade over 11,000 feet, I think . . . way out on the Tonahutu, about three miles past where you're staying at Granite Falls. It's worth the climb to get there, especially if you enjoy fishing like I do."

"I don't know . . . none of us are really fishermen," I confessed.

"Oh, well that's alright, just go up for the scenery then! Haynach's one of the prettiest places in the park, if you ask me. It doesn't get a lot of foot-traffic, but that's the best part."

A born and raised Coloradoan, the man was an experienced hiker who'd been coming out to Rocky Mountain National Park for the better part of the last fifty years. On top of that, he and his wife were now retired and lived right down the road in Grand Lake. The park was practically their backyard. If anyone could give us some insider advice on where to go, it was this guy.

"Just be careful of the snow," he cautioned. "This early in the season there's no telling what you'll run into up there. If it's too deep, don't screw around with it . . . it can be easy to get lost, and it's dangerous to get off-trail in the mountains."

Finishing up with our paperwork, the ranger handed us our permits and called for the next in line.

"Well, thanks for the tip," I told him as we turned to leave. "If we head up that way, I promise we'll be careful."

\*    \*    \*

**"WELL, SHOULD** we take that old dude's advice and go check out that lake?" Nick asked as we finished up our lunch.

"I mean, what else are we going to do here?"

*"Yeah, let's go do some exploring,"* said Chris, eagerly popping up to his feet. For a guy who was unsure of whether he'd like the whole hiking and camping thing and was planning on returning his used-boots when he got back home, he now seemed to be having the best time of all of us.

But standing up to grab my pack, I could immediately tell that something was off. Like flipping a switch, my body, which earlier that morning had kept a brisk pace on the trail, suddenly felt fatigued and heavy. And my mind, which had been laughing and telling jokes, seemed foggy as if I were sleepwalking.

After ten days on the road and on the trail, I'd finally hit a wall – and I'd hit it hard.

Leaving much of our gear and supplies back at camp in the interest of traveling light, Chris and Nick took the lead. After acclimating to the trail last night and this morning, the two of them were starting to get their hiking legs, and without the burden of a full pack they were now moving swiftly. My hiking legs, on the other hand, were about to fall off the hinges. It took all that I had not to fall behind as we began our trek towards the lake.

Within minutes we could hear the low, static rumble of Granite Falls growing louder as we approached. From the sound alone we could immediately tell it was going to be spectacular, and sure enough, it didn't disappoint. In the prime of late spring, with millions of gallons of fresh snowmelt surging down from the mountains' higher elevations, the onslaught of whitewater was so powerful and relentless that we could actually feel it rushing by. Standing at the edge as it cascaded over and around massive dark boulders in its path, it was the same sensation one might feel standing inches away from a freight train as it whizzes by on the tracks.

Leaving the falls and continuing on, we now settled into a relaxed but steady pace, as the terrain soon flattened out and abruptly transformed from lush woods to a charred graveyard of burnt trees left behind from a wildfire that swept through this section of the park two years earlier. Passing through the remnants of the blaze, we eventually arrived at a rocky outcrop perched high above a large grassy meadow. It was the perfect place to pause for a little break, and as we took off our packs and sat down on the flat rock ledge, I noticed the stone was pleasantly warm to the touch under the intense rays of the sun. I suddenly felt quite relaxed, and lying down on the warm granite, I pulled the brim of my ball cap low over my eyes while Chris and Nick chatted and surveyed the meadow below.

*     *     *

**SOMETIME LATER** Chris nudged me awake. "Hey, Rob," he said, softly shaking my shoulder.

*"Huuhhh?"* I responded groggily, brushing the cap off my face and squinting hard into the sun as I looked up towards him. It took me a few seconds to get my bearings and realize where I was.

"You look terrible," he said staring down at me. "You were passed out for like fifteen minutes. You alright, man?"

"Oh yeah . . . never felt better," I said, wiping a thin stream of drool from the corner of my mouth.

"I was just resting my eyes," I added unconvincingly, as he

helped me back up to my feet.

Back on the move, the three of us continued pressing higher into the mountains. Leaving behind the remains of the charred forest, we returned to deeply green woodlands where the pleasant fragrance of pine again hung in the air. Quickly falling into a comfortable rhythm on the trail, we in time reached an unexpectedly beautiful, long tumbling waterfall which we crossed by way of a slick wooden plank that spanned just inches above the fast-moving waterline. Watching Chris and Nick cautiously make their way before me, I overconfidently strode out onto the span and halfway across felt as my boot slipped out from under me, only narrowly avoiding what would have been a nasty and painful fall on the rocks below.

"Man, you're having a rough afternoon," joked Nick, as I joined them on the other side.

Unfortunately, things were about to get worse . . . for all of us.

\*     \*     \*

**NOW AT** an elevation of well over 10,000 feet, we soon began to notice a distinct chill in the air which had us stopping to reach into our packs for our light jackets. Minutes later, rounding a bend in the path, we watched as the trail before us disappeared under a blanket of glimmering white that stretched on as far as the eye could see. We had officially reached the snowline.

At first, it was barely even an inconvenience. Only an inch or two deep, we were easily able to march ahead through a narrow hollow cut into the woods where the trail was hidden, but clearly underfoot. It was actually quite beautiful. But eventually exiting the hollow, our clearly defined path gave way to a stretch of woods where it was now impossible to discern which way to go next. There were at least a half-dozen potential passages through the trees, any one of which (or none of which) could be the trail. There was simply no way to tell.

"Um, so where do we go now, guys?" asked Chris, perplexed like the rest of us.

The obvious answer was to turn around, cut our losses, and trace back to the main trail rather than run roughshod through the mountains where we had no earthly idea what we were doing or where we were going. Like the old man had said back at the visitor center, *"Be careful of the snow . . . it can be easy to get lost, and it's dangerous to get off-trail in the mountains."*

Yes, turning around would have been the smart thing to do.

Thus, it should come as no surprise that we decided to push on.

*     *     *

**DECIDING TO** follow a narrow creek that we hoped would lead us to the lake, we immediately received a rude awakening – even if this was the way up to Haynach (and trust me, that was a big "if") it was going to be damn difficult getting there. Whereas moments before the snow underfoot had only been a few inches deep and nothing more than a minor inconvenience, within a matter of minutes it had already risen to our knees. Soon after, it had amassed all the way up to our thighs. No longer were we walking on top of it, so much as quite literally plowing through it on a long and laboring upward ascent.

With loose snow collapsing around us with every step forward, our waterproof boots proved futile against that which made its way in at our ankles and immediately began to melt and drain down to the soles of our shoes. Expending tons of energy just to make the smallest progress, and now sloshing around in wet cotton socks, our group morale was quickly plummeting. Rather than the happy-go-lucky hikers we'd been earlier, enjoying a beautiful spring day in the mountains, we now looked more like the worn and battered soldiers of Napoleon's ill-prepared French army as it retreated from Moscow and proceeded to freeze to death in the harsh Russian winter. In other words, for those of you not so historically inclined, it fucking sucked.

Miserably wading through the snow, things only got worse as we were now funneled into a dense thicket of brush and fallen trees along the creek. Here the snow was much shallower, but bushwhacking through thorn bushes and crawling on hands and knees under tree limbs, we'd merely traded in one set of difficulties for another. Suddenly, I began to seriously question the sanity of continuing ahead under such miserable conditions. Was a small, inconsequential lake up in the mountains really worth all this trouble?

But just as we were about to throw in the towel and put an end to the madness, we finally caught a break.

Exiting the canopy of trees along the stream, the snow underfoot abruptly changed. Rather than the wet and heavy variety we'd been slogging through for the past hour, it was suddenly comprised of a sturdy, frozen icy crust on the surface. At some point this snow had melted during the day and later refrozen at night, meaning that for the first time in ages, we were actually walking on top of it rather than trudging through it. For us, this was the equivalent of a minor miracle.

Squinting hard in the face of a blazing white glare which reflected off the surface, we continued our climb in a single-file line – Chris in the front, I in the middle, and Nick in the back. In spite of everything we'd endured to get here, the three of us were now flying up the mountain at a pace that only moments before would have seemed impossible.

And then, nearing the top of a large rise in the terrain, we saw it – an unassuming, narrow mountain valley in the distance. From this vantage, we could plainly see this was home to the source of the stream we'd been following.

"That's gotta be the valley we're looking for, isn't it?" asked Chris excitedly. "The lake has to be up there, right?"

"I think you're right, bud. Look at that," I said pointing into the distance.

There, up ahead, stood a small, lonely wooden sign posted in the ground. It was the first trail marker we'd seen in over an hour.

Breaking out in wild, spontaneous celebration, the three of us hooted and hollered like sailors lost at sea who'd just caught our first sight of dry land. We were going to make it after all. With the sign facing the opposite direction, it left little doubt we had indeed taken a backwards approach on our route, but by this point it didn't matter. We had somehow found our way.

*Maybe this wasn't such a bad idea after all,* I thought to myself. I had to admit, it did kind of feel like an adventure.

But no sooner had we finally found confidence we would reach our goal did the mountain again throw a nasty wrench in our plans. With Chris leading the charge uphill, without warning he unexpectedly plunged through the surface of the snow, his left leg buried up to the hip while the rest of his body remained on the surface.

*"Damn,"* he muttered as he pulled himself out and regained his footing on both feet, "this stuff is deep under here."

Perhaps ten yards further, the same thing happened to Nick. It was as if both of them had been casually walking along the sidewalk and unexpectedly stepped into an open manhole cover.

We were *postholing*, a term used by high-elevation hikers to describe the common springtime nuisance of crashing through soft snow and leaving behind a long, narrow hole resembling what you might dig to place a fencepost in the ground. With a loud grunt, Nick pulled himself out, and we again resumed. Suddenly, I wasn't feeling so good about things again. Was it going to be like this the rest of the way?

"If this keeps up much longer guys, we might want to think about turning around," I said nervously. "This could be . . ."
*WHOOSH!*

Without warning I plummeted through the surface, momentarily in a state of panicked freefall. Instinctively throwing my arms out, they slammed into the snow catching my fall, but not before my chin bounced jarringly off its cold icy crust. Briefly knocked out of my senses, tiny blurs of light hovered across my vision as I realized the entire right side of my body was completely engulfed up to my chest.

*"Holy shit!"* shouted Chris, who'd heard the ordeal and spun

around to find me half-swallowed by the snow. *"Are you ok?!"*

He looked horrified.

Groggily, I crawled out of the hole. "Uh, yeah . . . I'm fine . . . I think," I answered unsteadily.

Prior to crashing through, I'd been walking next to a large boulder protruding from the snow. Looking down into the cavern left behind from my fall, I could now see the base of that same boulder easily *six or seven feet down*. Forget postholes – this was a full-fledged sinkhole.

Suddenly my heart was racing, as the gravity of what we were doing started to sink in. For the first time on my journey, I felt as if I might actually be doing something really stupid that could get me and my friends hurt. Even in the Lamar Valley, when I'd had my minor breakdown from fear of the wolves, I knew deep down my fears were mostly imagined. But this time, they weren't just in my head – they were very real and potentially very serious. Every year dozens of people die being reckless in the mountains, and I wasn't about to be one of them.

"This snow is way deeper than we thought, guys" I said gravely. "I could have fallen in up past my head . . . hell, I could have been completely buried."

Both Chris and Nick remained still, frozen in place, afraid to move lest they go crashing through the surface as well.

"We need to get the hell out of here, *now*," I added, stating what was already painfully obvious.

It didn't matter that we'd come this far, and it didn't matter that after so much effort we'd made it so close. After what had just happened, none of us were willing to take another single step up this mountain.

And just like that, the quest for Haynach was over. And for all practical purposes, so was my journey through the West.

# 24.

**BY THE** time we arrived back at camp, it was already early evening, and we were all pretty well beat from a day that in total covered nearly ten miles on the trail. In particular, the trek through the deep snow up by Haynach had been particularly grueling. With our feet still soaked, we sat down and pulled off our cold, wet socks with great relief and hung them in nearby branches to dry. But without an extra pair, and with a brisk evening chill setting in, I was soon forced to slip my bare feet back into my boots and spent the remainder of the night wriggling my toes in a futile effort to keep warm.

Eating dinner later on, I could barely keep my eyes open as the full force of the past ten days came crashing down on me like boulders from the mountainside. Desperately needing sleep, I wanted nothing more than to crawl into our tent and curl up in my not-so-warm sleeping bag for a long night's rest. I'd need all the energy I could muster up for the long haul back to the car the next day, as we retraced our route back to the trailhead. Right now, the thought of it seemed utterly daunting, though thankfully this time it would all be slightly downhill.

But before I could go to bed, it was time for a little celebration. For our last night in the woods, we'd each brought along some drinks, which Nick had just retrieved from the bear canisters and was now happily passing around. And all at once it hit me – this was it. Tomorrow I'd be back on the interstate, driving east through the night across the Great Plains, on my way back home to Iowa.

I couldn't help but reminisce. From the Smoky Mountains of Tennessee, to the Tetons of Jackson Hole, the wild canyons and valleys of Yellowstone, the snow-covered peaks of Colorado, and the countless places in between – the whole trip had been a whirlwind. Sure, I was coming back home to all of the uncertainty in my life that had taken me here in the first place. But for the first time in a long time, I felt invigorated and ready for whatever challenges lie ahead. If I could make it from the Appalachians to the Rockies in one piece, in spite of all my screw-ups and mistakes along the way, I knew I'd be able to make it through just about anything.

"Rob, I have an announcement . . ." said Chris, jarring me from my thoughts. He paused to heighten the suspense.

". . . I'm keeping my rental boots!"

"*Really?!*" I replied laughing. "That's awesome! So you must've had a good time after all?"

"Are you kidding? I had a *great* time. This was one of the coolest things I've ever done in my life. There's something about being out here in the mountains, away from everything and everyone. I don't know how to explain it, man. The whole time it was just . . . *exciting.*"

"Even the part up by Haynach this afternoon?" I asked jokingly.

"Especially that," he replied. "I mean, you were the one who almost died up there . . . not me," he added with a smirk.

And now with Chris, Nick, and I huddled together at our campsite, listening to the roar of the Tonahutu Creek in the background as the night grew dark, the three of us grabbed our drinks and raised them in the air as Chris delivered a fitting final toast.

"To one hell of an adventure, guys," he said as we all clinked our bottles.

Taking a long, deep draw of my whiskey, I smiled . . . I couldn't have said it any better myself.

# ABOUT THE AUTHOR

After a career of coaching small-college football that took him across the country, Rob Erwin now writes full time about his travels through America's eclectic small towns and remote wild places. Born and raised in rural Illinois, he currently lives in Bettendorf, Iowa, with his wife, Kellie. His next book, *Lost on the Rails*, is slated for release in December 2017.

87010444R00111

Made in the USA
Middletown, DE
01 September 2018